Learn to Swim in a Weekend

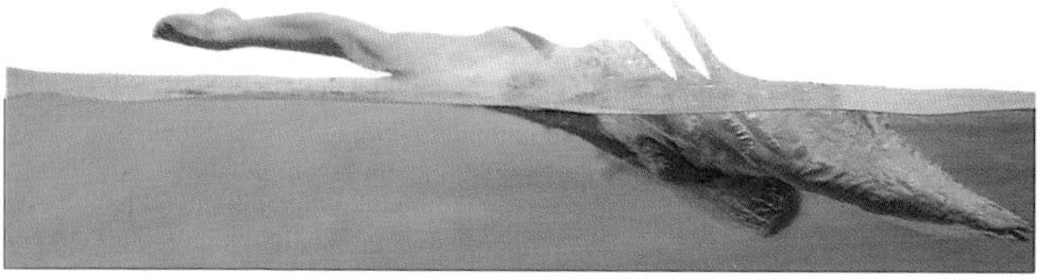

LEARN TO SWIM IN A WEEKEND

SHARRON DAVIES
with JAMES HARRISON

EDITORIAL CONSULTANT
ROSA GALLOP

Photography by Chris Stevens

ALFRED A. KNOPF
New York
1992

A DORLING KINDERSLEY BOOK

This edition is a Borzoi Book published in 1992 by Alfred A. Knopf, Inc.,
by arrangement with Dorling Kindersley.

Art Editor Kevin Williams
Senior Art Editor Tina Vaughan
Project Editor Ann Kay
Managing Editor Sean Moore
Production Controller Deborah Wehner

Library of Congress Cataloging-in-Publication Data
Davies, Sharron.
Learn to swim in a weekend / Sharron Davies with James Harrison: photography, Chris Stevens
p. cm.
Includes index.
ISBN 0-679-41276-X
1. Swimming. I. Harrison, James. II. Title.
GV837.D27 1992
797.2'1--dc20 91-58626
CIP

Reproduced by Colourscan, Singapore
Printed and bound by Arnoldo Mondadori, Verona, Italy

First American Edition

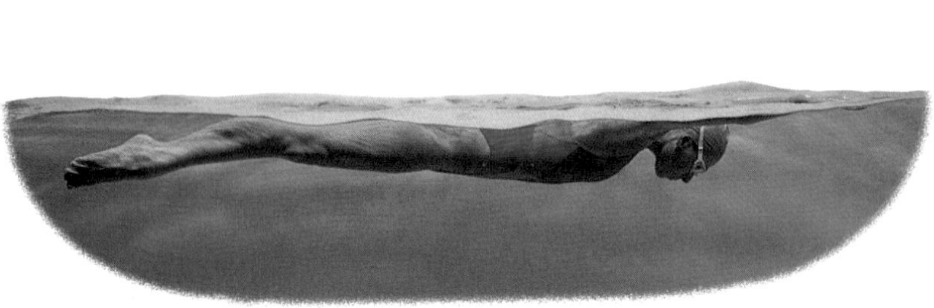

CONTENTS

INTRODUCTION

LEARN TO SWIM IN A WEEKEND was an ideal opportunity for me – along with Dorling Kindersley – to present a superb pictorial guide to the sport, with exciting split-level shots that make each skill easy to follow. In this book, straightforward, step-by-step instructions will show you how to gain water confidence, learn the basic strokes, create a good swimming style, and use the correct equipment.

This book can help a total novice who has always wanted to learn to swim, but has perhaps felt uneasy in and around water, just as much as it provides valuable advice for the experienced swimmer who wishes to find ways of improving his or her technique. However, remember that to do anything well, it will always take time, effort, and more than a little patience.

I've been swimming competitively since I was eight years old, and, over the years, I have seen many changes and developments in

techniques, and in the thinking behind those techniques. Through all of these changes, certain fundamental principles have remained the same, and it is these that I have stressed throughout *Learn to Swim in a Weekend.* These points are simple, sensible, and easy to remember – that taking water from in front of you and pushing it behind will propel you forwards; that a streamlined shape moves faster than any other; that your legs form a powerful rear "engine"; and that bringing control, strength, and good technique together will create a style that displays both grace and efficiency.

While these basic pointers can help all levels of swimmer, you will find, whatever your abilities, that there are hints, tips, and drills aimed specifically at you, in the hope that you will learn to love a sport that is excellent for your all-round health, and that people of every age can thoroughly enjoy.

SHARRON DAVIES

PREPARING FOR THE WEEKEND

To do anything well, you must make the right kind of preparations

WHETHER YOU WANT TO LEARN to be a competent recreational swimmer, or improve your technique to competition standard, go over the following checklist before embarking on your weekend course. The most important factor to begin with is health and fitness. If you are at all worried about your health – especially if you have problems with your breathing, ears, or eyes – then visit your doctor first. It is also worth limbering up, either at home, or by the pool, before you go into the water. Simple stretching exercises are a good start (see pp.18-19). Exercises such as sit-ups strengthen the stomach, the body's "core" – a strong stomach helps the rest of your body to work better. Do this course in the controlled setting of a

GETTING ON GOGGLES
Many swimming skills require you to immerse your face in water, or look where you're going under the water. You may find this more comfortable, especially as eyes can be easily irritated by chlorine, if you wear goggles. Always put the eyepieces over your eyes *before* putting the strap around the back of your head (p.17).

STRETCH
Flexibility is vital for successful swimming. Any standing pre-swim exercises, such as this side-stretch, should be done with slightly bent knees. If your legs are too stiff, you could strain your back and knees (pp.18-19).

swimming pool, rather than the ocean; check which pool in your area has the best facilities for your needs (see pp.12-13). You must also equip yourself properly. The financial outlay is low compared to other sports (see pp.10-11, 16-17), but shop around – it pays to get the right gear, such as a swimsuit designed for swimming, rather than for sunbathing. *Words in **bold** are given further explanation in the glossary (pp.92-93).*

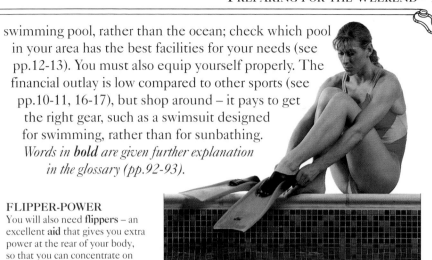

FLIPPER-POWER
You will also need **flippers** – an excellent **aid** that gives you extra power at the rear of your body, so that you can concentrate on moving the front. Check that your pool allows flippers (many don't, although some may relent during quieter periods).

SWIMMING GEAR
With most swimming gear, it's worth taking spare items – swimming goggles, for example, are damaged especially quickly by chlorine. Being immersed in water is hard on your skin and hair too – take along good-quality soap, moisturizer, shampoo, and conditioner (pp.10-11).

WHAT YOU NEED

Selecting the right swimwear and swimming accessories

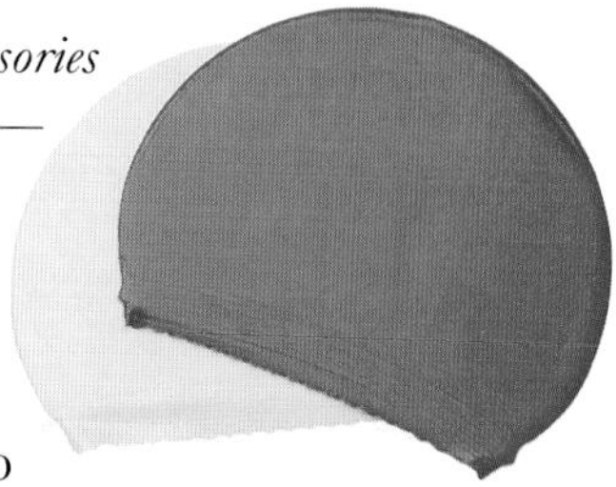

CHOOSE SWIMWEAR that is comfortable and stretchy, and allows a wide range of movement. Lightweight, non-absorbent fabrics, and a snug fit, will ensure that you don't get waterlogged. You may also want to take **aids**, to make practice easier and more fun. Rinse everything out afterwards, so that the chlorine (which is a bleach) doesn't rot your gear.

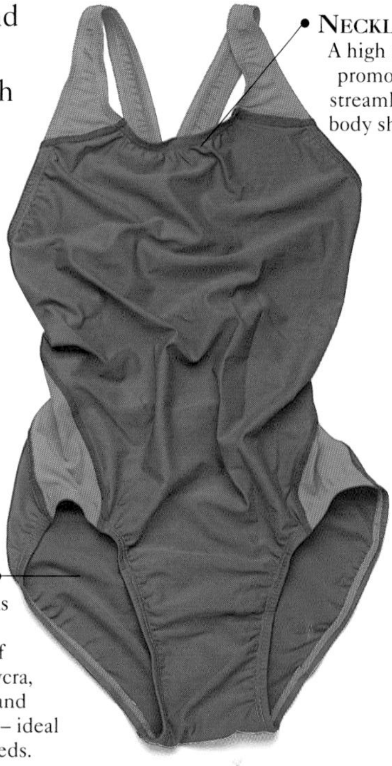

NECKLINE A high neck promotes a streamlined body shape.

SWIMWEAR

Try swimwear on before you buy, and choose styles that aren't too skimpy. Some pools insist that you wear a cap, to prevent loose hair from clogging up their filters. Swimming caps are made of rubber; sprinkle with talcum powder to stop the rubber sticking to itself after use.

FABRIC Most trunks and suits are made of stretchy Lycra, or a Lycra and cotton mix – ideal for your needs.

BAG Take a kit bag with several waterproof pockets, to keep wet and dry items apart.

COLORS Avoid colors, such as red and white, that go transparent when wet. Try to go for mid to dark blues, or black.

Dry off with a large cotton towel

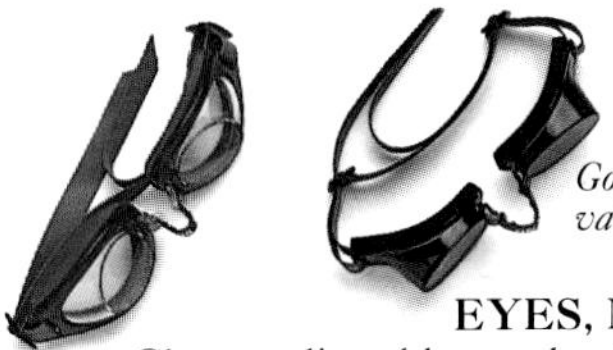

Nose clip

Goggles come in various styles

Molded ear plugs

EYES, NOSE, EARS

Choose adjustable goggles. If you wish, use plugs and clips to stop water soaking your ears, or rushing up your nose.

BODY-CARE

Pack shower gel and shampoo. Also, alcohol-based ear drops dry out ears and so prevent infection; skin moisturizer, hair conditioner, and soothing eye drops combat the effects of chlorine.

AIDS TO SUCCESSFUL SWIMMING

GETTING EXTRA HELP

Flippers, **floats**, and other buoyancy **aids** can be a worthwhile investment. For example, floats can keep you buoyant while you concentrate on your arm action or leg action (see pp.16-17, 28-33). Avoid cheap floats, as they break up easily.

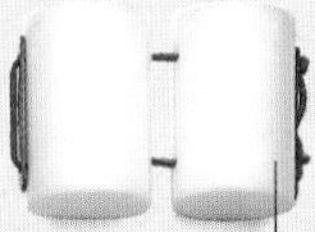

PULL-BUOY

This **aid** goes between your legs, keeping you afloat while you do arm-only **drills**.

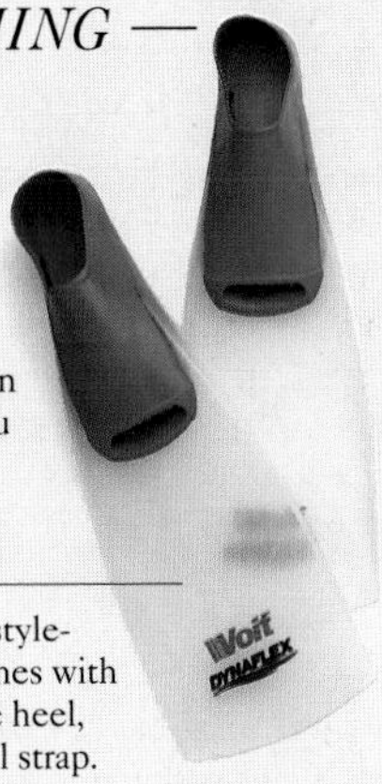

FLIPPERS

These are excellent style-enhancers. Choose ones with a complete, shoe-like heel, rather than just a heel strap.

KICKBOARDS

Use big **kickboards** (or "kick **floats**") for legs-only **drills**; put smaller ones between your knees for arm-only drills.

JACKET

Used to gain basic water confidence, buoyancy jackets have pockets which contain small **floats**. Remove floats as less buoyancy is required.

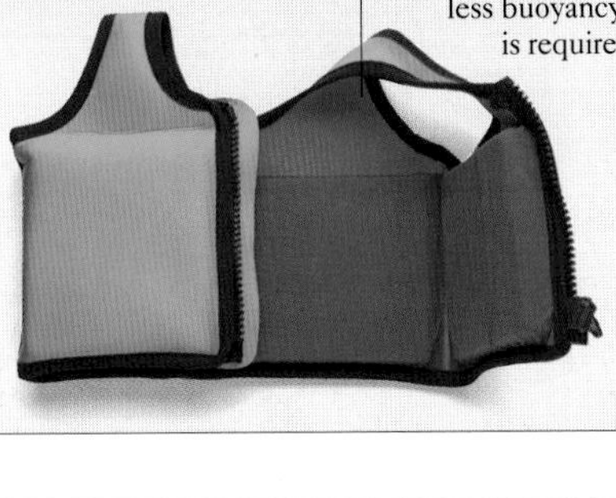

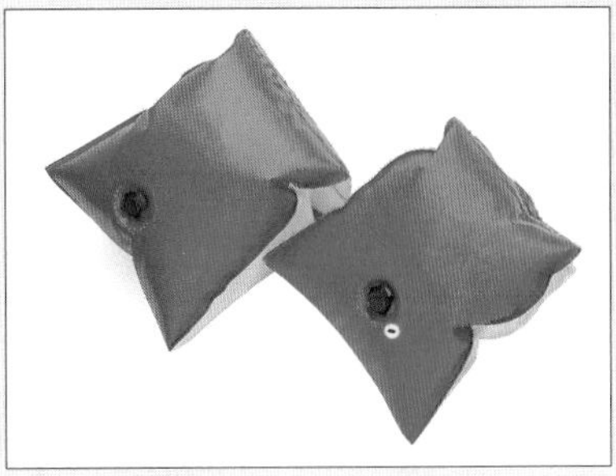

AVOID WATER WINGS

These are really only helpful for keeping toddlers and babies upright. Don't rely on them – they restrict arm movement, and encourage the wrong position for swimming.

AT THE POOL

Your swimming will benefit if you choose a pool with certain basic features

LOOK FOR CLEAN, supervised changing areas, alert poolside staff, and well-kept **aids** (including safety aids such as lifebuoys). Water depths and safety instructions should be clearly marked. The water temperature (preferably about 27°C/80°F) should be on display, and, if chlorine affects you adversely, check whether the pool uses ozone as a water purifier. For a reasonable amount of stroke practice, choose a 25-m (80-ft), six-lane pool, or at least one that has a separate, laned area.

LEISURE POOLS
These are for fun, not serious swimming. Their gently sloping shallows, waterfalls (right), slides, and general playground atmosphere, make them better for children, or for simply getting used to water, than for teaching or learning strokes.

TUITION TIME

Right: Most good pools offer classes for all ages and abilities (and disabilities), with fully qualified instructors. Group activity can make learning easier, particularly if you are learning from scratch.

CHILDREN'S POOLS

Below: Many swimming pools have a separate shallow children's pool. Games that promote water confidence, such as standing in a circle and splashing water, can be an excellent start to a child's swimming program.

SWIMMING IN THE OCEAN

BEING BUOYANT

Although it's best to do this course in a pool, learning to swim in the ocean is easier for some due to the extra buoyancy that salt water gives. You may also find it a more invigorating setting than a chemically controlled pool. As attendants are not close by, never swim alone. Check weather and tide conditions, depths, and entry and exit points. Stay parallel to the shore – don't swim out to sea.

WHY SWIMMING?

... For health and safety, fitness and fun

MOST PEOPLE ENJOY being around water, so you should know how to swim as a safety measure – the younger you learn, the better. Swimming is the perfect example of a sport, leisure pursuit, and fitness activity rolled into one, and open to all. Children and their grandparents, athletes, pregnant women, those with disabilities – anyone can find something beneficial to mind or body in a water environment. But, above all, swimming should be fun – enjoy it.

MEETING EVERYONE'S NEEDS

HELPING YOUR HEALTH

Swimming is excellent for overall fitness:
- it improves stamina and co-ordination;
- it exercises more muscle groups than any other sport;
- it gets your heart and lungs working more efficiently, which boosts the circulation of oxygen around your body;
- it provides natural buoyancy while you exercise, minimizing strain on the body.

SPECIAL NEEDS

Like no other sport, swimming caters to special needs. For example, it can be enjoyed by asthmatics and epileptics, and those with all kinds of physical disabilities benefit from water's natural support.

PREGNANCY

Swimming provides relief from some of the weight and strain of late pregnancy, and can make women more supple for the birth.

LATER IN LIFE

You're never too old for a gentle swim. Hardy 70-, 80-, and 90-year-olds can even enter Masters events (see p.83).

BABIES AND TODDLERS

Young children gain confidence, exercise, and co-ordination. They must be watched carefully and encouraged constantly.

OTHER SPORTS

Learning to swim allows you to take part confidently and safely in a wide range of water sports. You may simply want to enjoy these on holiday or at weekends, or go further and enter competitions.

SETTING YOUR SIGHTS HIGH

There are three Olympic sports for which you must be able to swim (apart from swimming itself). 1. Diving (below). 2. Water Polo (below right), requiring good buoyancy and swimming skills. 3. Synchronized swimming (right), for which you need good **sculling** skills and stamina. Many pools run clubs for these sports.

WIND AND WATER

Above and Above Left: To enjoy windsurfing and water-skiing fully, you must have learned at least the basics of swimming (as in Skills 1-3 of this book). You don't want to be panic-stricken every time you fall into the water.

ON THE SURF

Left: True surfing requires a high degree of swimming competence. You must be able to swim strongly to get over the crashing surf, and to cope with the biggest of tumbles.

SWIMMING AIDS

Helping you to float and stay horizontal in the water

THERE ARE MANY SWIMMING **aids** on the market today. While some can help the learning process along, others may be a hindrance because you can become too reliant on them. **Flippers** (also called fins), **kickboards**, and **pull-buoys** – all shown here – are valuable because they help to keep you horizontal in the water.

FLIPPERS

Wearing **flippers** is useful because it helps to keep your body horizontal in the water, and gives you far greater flexibility, especially in the ankles. This flexibility is essential for kicking movements, where flippers act as an extension of your legs, pushing you more forcefully through the water. Also, for less confident swimmers, flippers can provide a feeling of both power and speed.

FLIPPER FIT
Put **flippers** on by pushing your feet in deep before securing the heel piece around the back of your foot. They must fit closely to be effective.

OUT OF THE WATER
It's easier to put **flippers** on out of the water, while sitting down and watching what you are doing.

LEG-POWER
Wearing flippers can really help your swimming – they can increase your leg power 2½ times. However, not all pools allow them, so check before you go.

TAKE-OFF
It's much easier to take **flippers** off in the water, but remember that they sink and be prepared to scoop them up.

FLOATS

Floats – such as **kickboards** and **pull-buoys** – help to keep you buoyant while you concentrate on one aspect of a particular stroke.

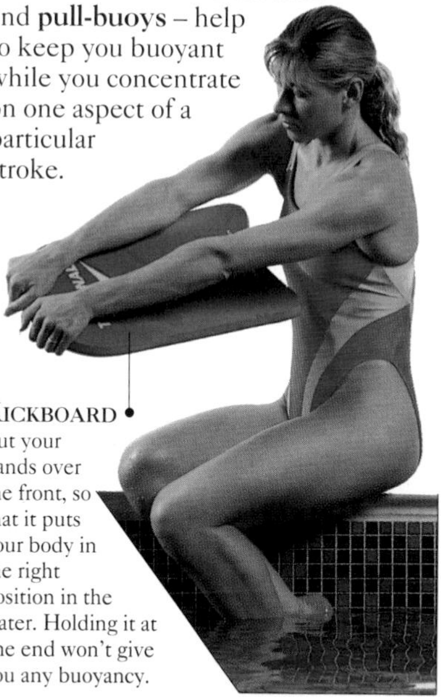

KICKBOARD
Put your hands over the front, so that it puts your body in the right position in the water. Holding it at one end won't give you any buoyancy.

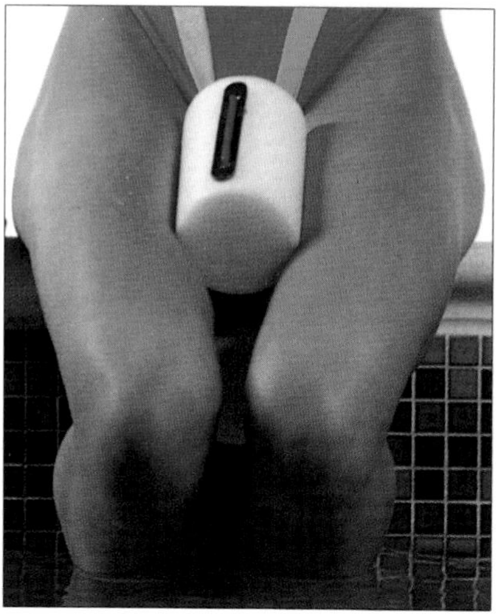

PULL-BUOY POWER
Both a learn-to-swim **aid** and an advanced training aid, **pull-buoys** keep your legs afloat and your body in the right position while you concentrate on your arm action. Put it between your legs and pull with your arms.

GOGGLES

Goggles let you see where you're going (and what your hands are doing) under the water and prevent chlorinated water from irritating your eyes.

1. To put your goggles on safely: Place the eyepieces on your eyes.

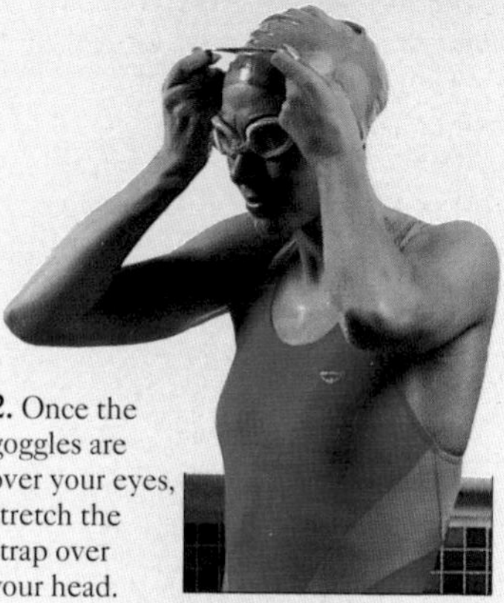

2. Once the goggles are over your eyes, stretch the strap over your head.

3. Adjust the strap to fit.

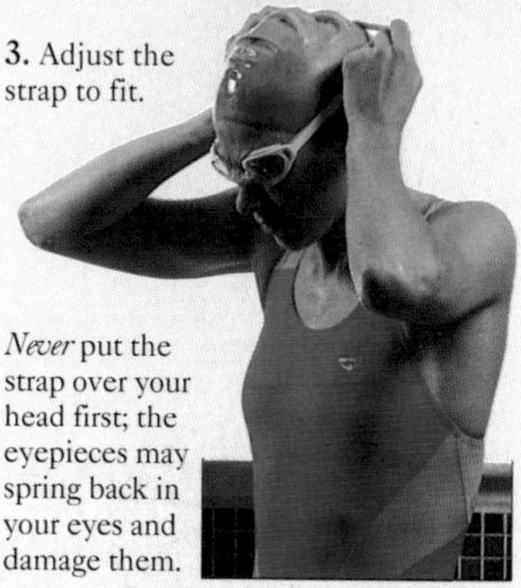

Never put the strap over your head first; the eyepieces may spring back in your eyes and damage them.

PRE-SWIM WARM-UP

Simple exercises to limber up the muscles used when swimming

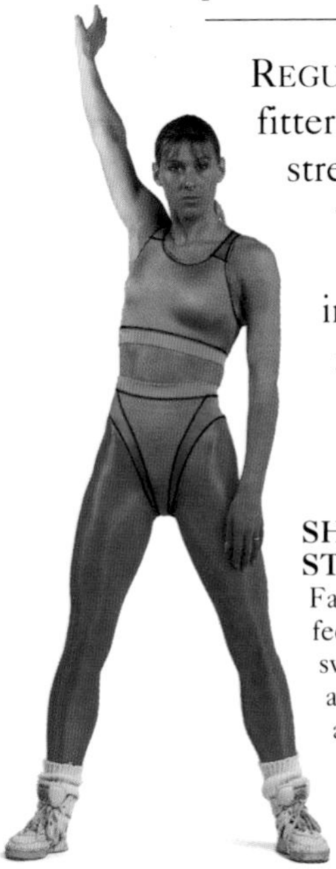

REGULAR, BASIC EXERCISE will make you that vital bit fitter for when you get into the water. These examples strengthen both heart and lungs, and the stretching will help to prevent possible day-to-day muscle injury (swimming itself isn't really prone to the injuries associated with land sports, because of the natural support of the water). Try these exercises before and after swimming; take them slowly, and gradually build up the amount you do.

SHOULDER STRETCH

Facing ahead, with feet apart, slowly swing each arm in as large a circle as possible, first forwards, then backwards. Feel the stretch in your shoulders.

HURDLE STRETCH

Seated as if hurdling, stretch at about 90° from the lower back to your front leg, then to your side leg. Touch tummy to top of leg, not nose to knee.

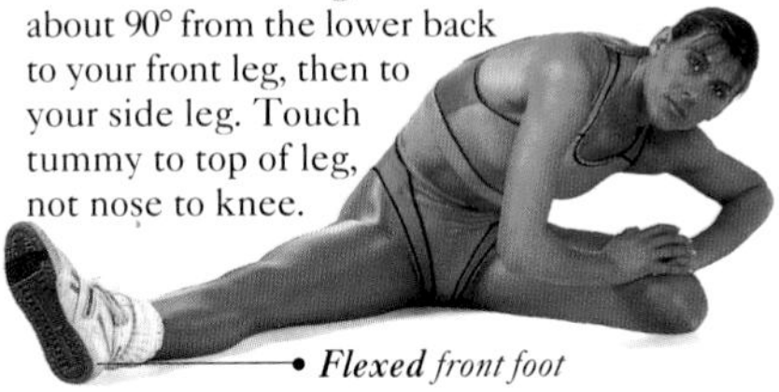

• ***Flexed** front foot*

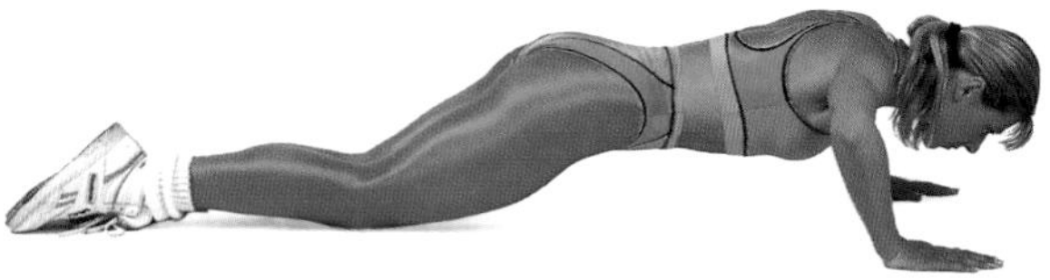

EASY PUSH-UP

Work your way up to a full press-up (foot of page) by supporting some of your weight on your knees before gradually moving your knees backwards and up.

SIT-UP

Slowly "squeeze" yourself up, stretching your arms out between your legs, and back down. Don't jerk your back, keep your feet on the floor, and sit on a towel or mat, if possible. Sit-ups are excellent stomach-toners.

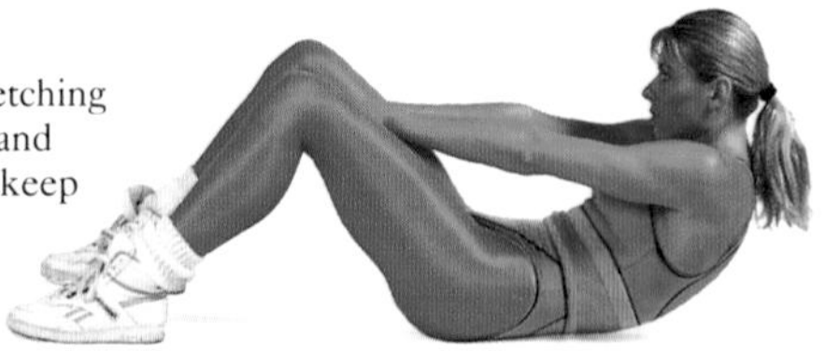

FEET
Spread your feet slightly for stability.

FULL PUSH-UP

With hands beneath shoulders, press your nose down to the floor, and up again. Keep your body in a straight line; don't stick your bottom up.

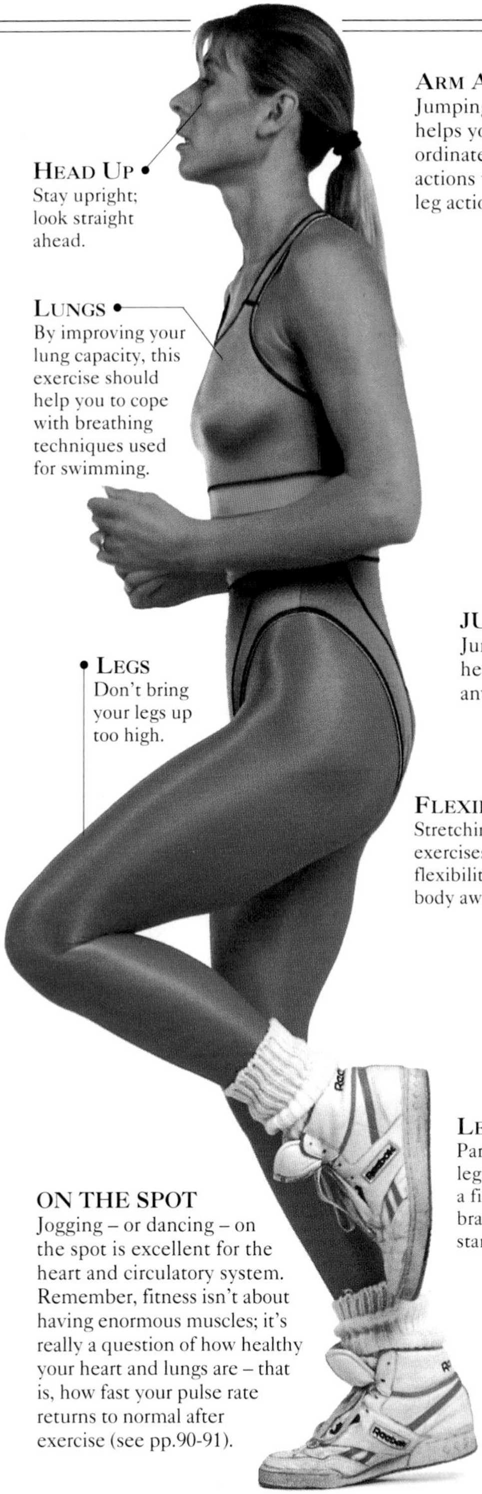

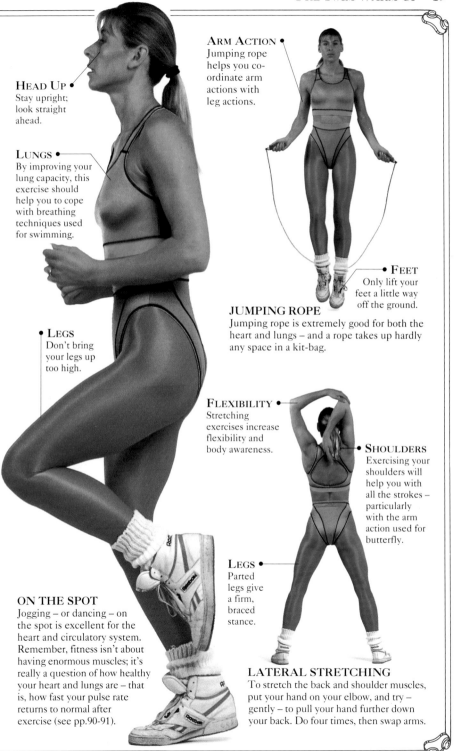

HEAD UP
Stay upright; look straight ahead.

LUNGS
By improving your lung capacity, this exercise should help you to cope with breathing techniques used for swimming.

LEGS
Don't bring your legs up too high.

ON THE SPOT

Jogging – or dancing – on the spot is excellent for the heart and circulatory system. Remember, fitness isn't about having enormous muscles; it's really a question of how healthy your heart and lungs are – that is, how fast your pulse rate returns to normal after exercise (see pp.90-91).

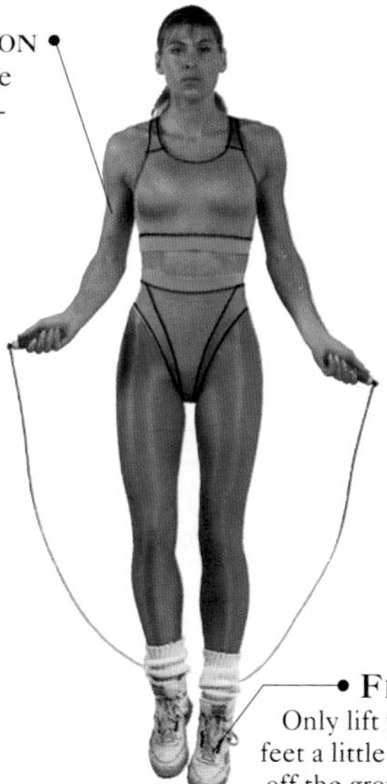

ARM ACTION
Jumping rope helps you co-ordinate arm actions with leg actions.

FEET
Only lift your feet a little way off the ground.

JUMPING ROPE

Jumping rope is extremely good for both the heart and lungs – and a rope takes up hardly any space in a kit-bag.

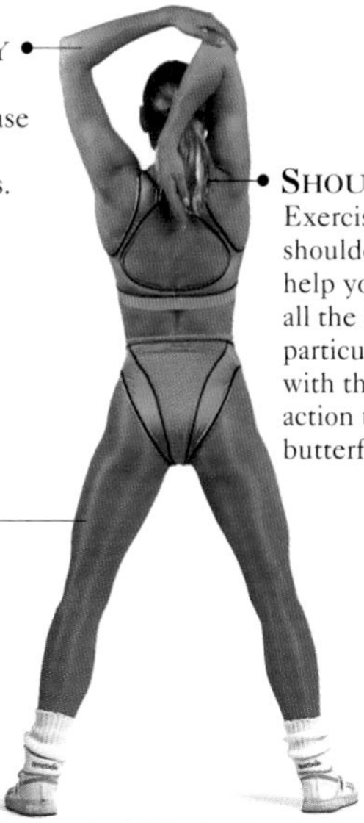

FLEXIBILITY
Stretching exercises increase flexibility and body awareness.

SHOULDERS
Exercising your shoulders will help you with all the strokes – particularly with the arm action used for butterfly.

LEGS
Parted legs give a firm, braced stance.

LATERAL STRETCHING

To stretch the back and shoulder muscles, put your hand on your elbow, and try – gently – to pull your hand further down your back. Do four times, then swap arms.

SETTING TARGETS

Make the most of learning by deciding on a realistic set of goals

YOUR SWIMMING WILL benefit if, before you start, you know exactly what you want to achieve – this applies to normal swimming sessions as well as to this course. As you go along, assess whether you are learning techniques correctly. Rather than rush on, eager to learn a new skill, go back a step, or a whole skill, if necessary.

Even if you feel that you should by-pass the water movement and stroke skills (Skills 1-7) and go straight to the turns, dives, and racing starts (Skills 8-10), think first. You may be able to do the front crawl, but do you have an efficient technique – as shown in this book? Can you breathe **bilaterally** (see p.55)? Until you can breathe properly, you shouldn't progress to the next skill. Similarly, good **flip turns** (see pp.68-73) depend on approaching the wall in the correct way, so don't tackle them until you have perfected your crawl.

Hopefully, this book will highlight your strengths and weaknesses. You may want to join a club in order to work on these – verbal coaching and a class environment can be extremely helpful, especially if you lack confidence. Don't get into bad habits that will be difficult to get rid of, and that will hinder your learning. And never make excuses because of age, sex, physique, or temperament!

COACHING
Decide whether you feel you would benefit from coaching. Most pools run classes for all abilities and some offer one-to-one coaching (above), if you're prepared for the extra cost.

ON YOUR OWN
You may decide that you want to practice by yourself most of the time, but seek the occasional advice of a teacher to check your progress and discuss technique points.

PERSONAL GOALS

Whenever you go swimming, if you want to progress at all, decide which aspect you need to work on: just the leg or arm action of a stroke, basic water confidence, timing, breathing, overall co-ordination, and so on. You will find it easier to tackle a skill if you break the skill down, practice its individual aspects, and then put it all together. Think about whether you could be helped by **aids**, for example to practice an arm or leg action (above right) or gain confidence in the water (below). Work slowly and smoothly, and think about what you're doing – aim to combine brains with "brawn".

LEG ACTIONS
If you decide that you want to work on a specific leg action (the breaststroke kick is shown in this picture), start off by practicing it without the arm action. Isolate any leg action by keeping the rest of the body buoyant with a **float**, as shown. (For arm actions, place a float between the legs.)

GAINING CONFIDENCE
If you can float face-down in the water, holding your breath, and stay relaxed, you have mastered a fundamental swimming skill.

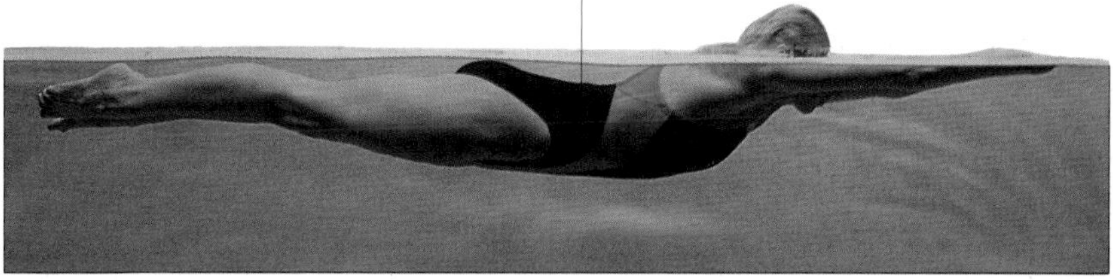

BACK TO BASICS
Be honest with yourself – do you need to go back to basics? You may well need to go back and practice the kind of rudimentary floating exercises shown above (see pp.24-33).

GET ORGANIZED
Right: It always helps to have some kind of plan of action, however basic. Shown here are ten key goals which you might like to work through to improve your abilities. Remember – never rush any program; take your swimming calmly and enjoy yourself. (See pp.90-91 for more advanced training schedules.)

Personal Planner

1	*Feel confident enough to swim a length of a stroke.*
2	*Get used to using swimming **aids** (see pp.16-17).*
3	*Improve your fitness; achieve a better heart recovery rate (see p.91).*
4	*Aim for a better style and technique on breaststroke, **backstroke**, and front crawl (see pp.34-59).*
5	*Feel confident about basic safety skills (see pp.86-87).*
6	*Learn to breathe **bilaterally** (see p.55).*
7	*Be able to do butterfly stroke correctly (see pp.60-67).*
8	*Master the front crawl **flip turn** (see pp.68-71).*
9	*Perfect your 200m individual medley – swimming all the strokes properly, and according to the correct rules (see pp.84-85, 93).*
10	*Aim to reach a competitive level (see pp.90-91).*

THE WEEKEND COURSE

Decide what you want to achieve over your weekend

A WIDE RANGE of swimming skills, covering many levels of ability, are spread over this two-day course. You may not want to be in the water for the length of time required to complete the course within two days. The best approach is to "dip in" at whatever level suits you. If you're a total novice, concentrate on Skills 1-3; only start the strokes (Skills 4-7), if you feel water-confident. You could save skills such as turns, dives, and racing starts (Skills 8-10) for another weekend, or spread the whole course over several weekends. But, whatever your ability, remember that feeling confident about what you're doing is the only real requirement.

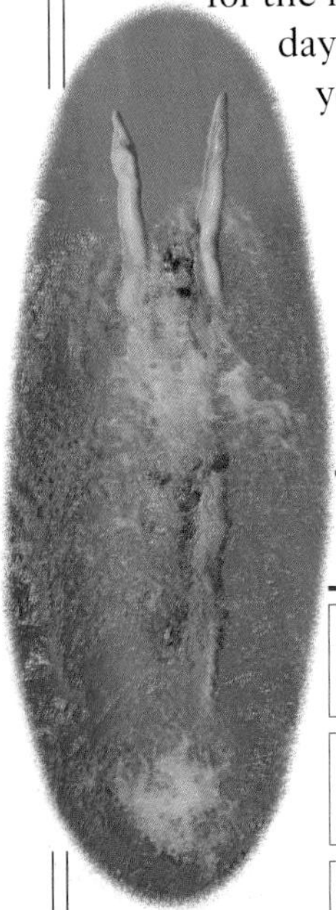

Double-arm backstroke

DAY 1		*Hours*	*Page*
SKILL 1	Getting into the water	½	24
SKILL 2	Buoyancy	½	28
SKILL 3	Learning to move	½	30
SKILL 4	Breaststroke	1	34
SKILL 5	Backstroke	1	44

Getting in and out of the pool

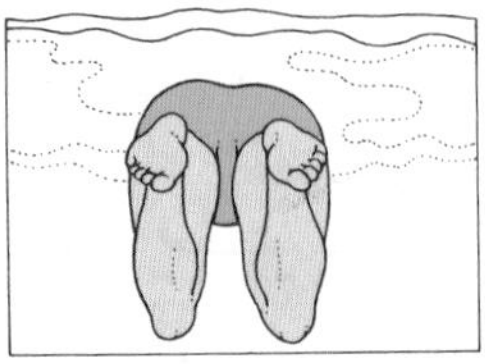

Breaststroke leg action

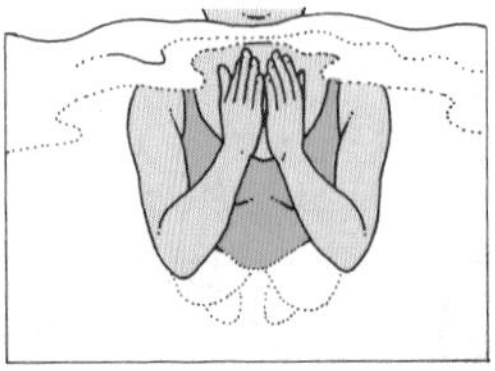

Breaststroke arm action

KEY TO SYMBOLS

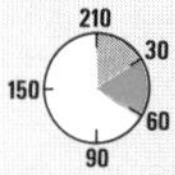

CLOCKS

Small clocks appear on the first page of each skill. The blue section shows how long you might spend on that skill, and where that skill fits into your day. For example, check the clock on p.28. The blue segment shows that ½ hour (shown as 30 minutes; all the times are shown on the clocks in minutes) should be set aside for Skill 2, and the grey segment shows that ½ hour was spent on the previous skill. But be flexible, use clocks as a guideline only, and settle in to a natural pace.

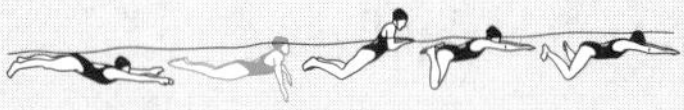

FIGURES

In each skill, the series of figures in the introduction, and by the steps, shows the number of steps in that skill. Blue figures identify the steps that are illustrated.

RATING SYSTEM •••••

Each skill is given a difficulty rating, from one bullet (•) for straightforward skills, to five bullets for skills that are more challenging.

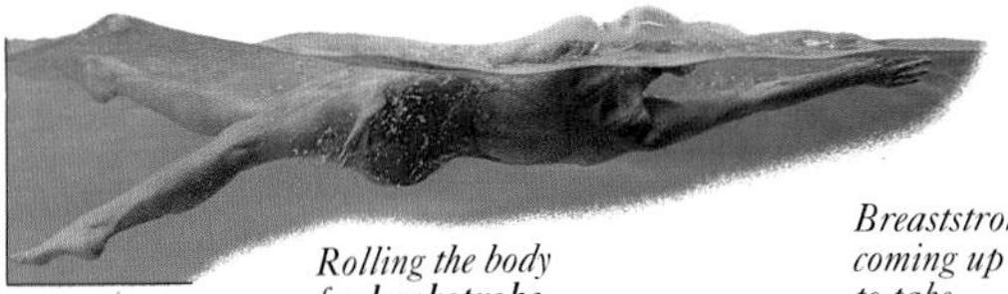

Rolling the body for ***backstroke***

Breaststroke: coming up to take a breath

DAY 2		*Hours*	*Page*
SKILL 6	Front crawl	1	52
SKILL 7	Butterfly	1	60
SKILL 8	Taking turns	¾	68
SKILL 9	Diving in	¾	74
SKILL 10	Racing start	½	78

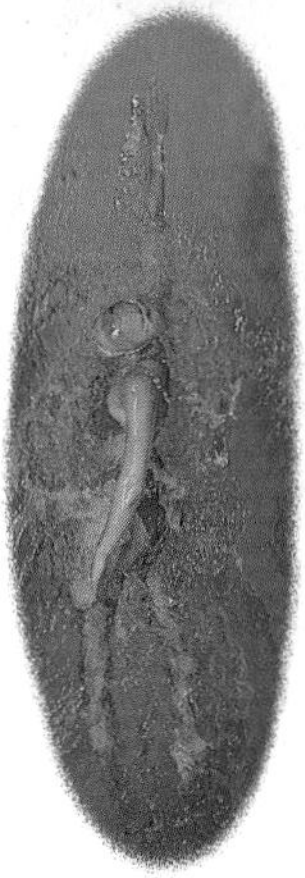

Reaching forward on front crawl

Using ***floats***

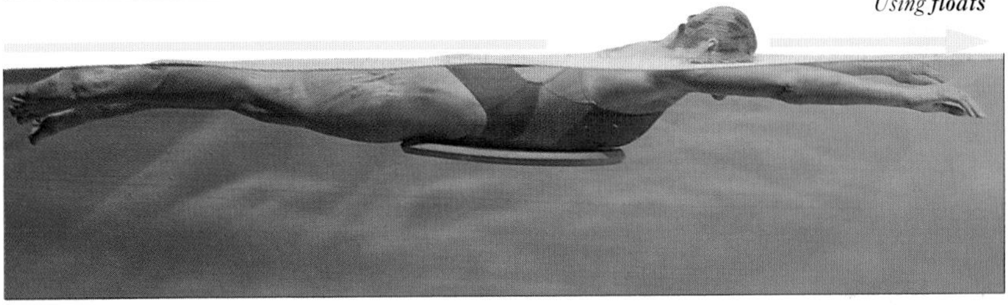

SKILL 1

GETTING INTO THE WATER

DAY 1

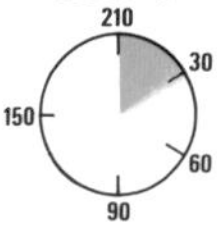

Definition: *Feeling at home in the water*

OVERCOMING ANY FEAR OF WATER needn't be daunting if you take it slowly. Find a warm pool (about 28°C/82°F), with a shallow end where you are not out of your depth and where no one is splashing about, and use the approaches shown here.

OBJECTIVE: To acquire a basic confidence in and around water. *Rating* •

USING STEPS

Always use the steps to enter the pool if you are at all uneasy in the water. Before you go down the steps, check the poolside water-level mark. Hold on to the rails and go down the pool steps backwards, slowly and carefully, until you touch the bottom of the pool. When standing on the bottom, the water should ideally be at about waist level. If necessary, have a **kickboard**, or some other kind of **float**, within easy reach.

BIT BY BIT
Going backwards, take one step at a time – don't be tempted to rush it.

RAIL
Hold on to the rail at all times.

LEGS
Keep your legs and feet totally relaxed; try not to tense up.

SAFE AND SOUND
Choose a part of the pool where you feel relaxed and unintimidated. Always check before going in that there are lifeguards beside the pool.

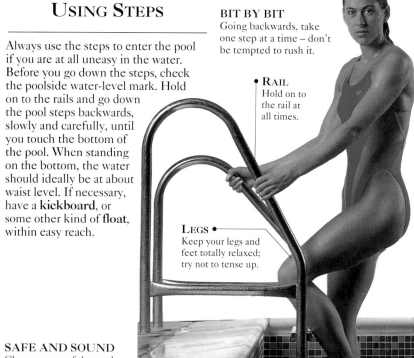

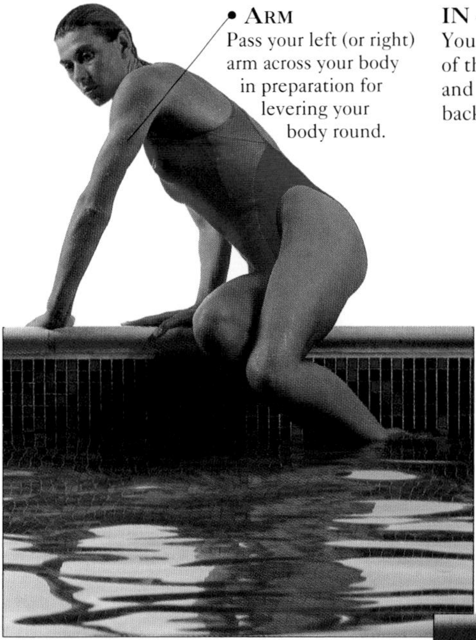

ARM
Pass your left (or right) arm across your body in preparation for levering your body round.

IN – AND OUT
You can also use this method for getting out of the pool. Put your hands up on the side and twist yourself round out of the water, back to a sitting position on the poolside.

TAKE THE WEIGHT
Take your body weight on your arms and hands as you gradually begin to lower yourself.

POOLSIDE ENTRY

Sit on the side at the shallow end of the pool, facing the water. With your hands on the side, slowly twist your body round and ease yourself in backwards. You will need some strength in your arms to take your weight.

MAKING AN EXIT

FOR THE MORE CONFIDENT
If you lack confidence, it's always best to use steps when getting in or out of the water; for those who are a little more relaxed near water, and who have quite strong arms, the method shown above is ideal. For people with fairly strong arms who are already perfectly water-confident, the method shown on the right is both a quick and effective way of getting out of (or into) a swimming pool. Hold onto the poolside from a position where you are facing out to the water, and simply push yourself up, using the strength in your arms, until you are sitting on the poolside.

ARM-POWER
Lever yourself up by using the power of your arm muscles.

SKILL 1

MAKING A SPLASH

This is a good way to get used to your face being wet. Stand in the shallows, with the steps in front of you. With your eyes closed, slowly start to throw water onto your face, gradually getting used to the feeling of having a wet face.

GO SLOWLY •
Splashing water on your face with your hands is a good way to lead into submerging your face (below). All swimming skills require you to get your face wet, and for most you need to be face-down in the water, in order to achieve a streamlined position in which you move easily, with economy of effort.

GOING DOWN

Once you're happy about splashing your face, try submerging it. Hold onto the poolside or hand-rail, and lower your face gradually into the water until it is totally submerged. Come back up almost immediately, and then do it again. Try simply bobbing your head in-and-out, in-and-out of the water, in a non-jerky fashion. When you feel more confident, go under for longer, holding your breath under the water. This will prepare you for swimming with an **oxygen deficit** and for exhaling under the water, and inhaling above the water – which is how you should breathe for the main strokes.

FINDING YOUR BEARINGS

DON'T PANIC
This routine builds the confidence you need for good underwater orientation. Left: submerge yourself, holding your breath, and open your eyes. You may feel better in goggles. Come up slowly. Right: Go back under, this time blowing bubbles by exhaling through your nose and mouth.

FLOATING

Now it's time for you to try floating "on top of" the water. Hold onto the poolside or steps, and, using your arm muscles for leverage, make yourself as flat on top of the water as you can. Float first on your front, and then on your back. Let the water come round your ears and practice submerging your head again. When you are feeling confident, try floating with a **kickboard** (see pp.28-29).

FEET
When on your back, hook your heels over the poolside steps.

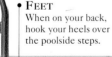

THE BEST HAND POSITION
Have one hand holding on higher up than the other. With both at the same height, it is very difficult to push the lower half of your body up so that your body is straight.

SKILL 2

BUOYANCY

DAY 1

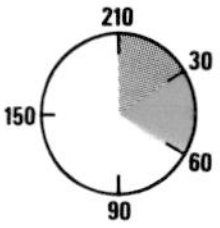

Definition: *Using* ***floats*** *to boost your buoyancy*

WE ALL FLOAT NATURALLY – not just because our bodies have less **density** than water, but also because the inhaled air in our lungs helps to keep us afloat. Even people whose muscle- or bone-weight makes them sink lower in the water, can float better if they hold their breath.

OBJECTIVE: To achieve a balanced body position in the water. *Rating* ••

FIRST FLOATS

Start out, in the shallow end of the swimming pool, with two simple floating positions: the first one "sitting down", and the second on your front. For the seated floating position, put a **kickboard** under your bottom, sit on it and **scull** (see p.31) with your hands. To float on your front, place a **float** under your stomach, and lie flat "on the top of" the water. This is the best swimming position, and the one that you want to be in when you come to do the main swimming strokes (see pp.34-67).

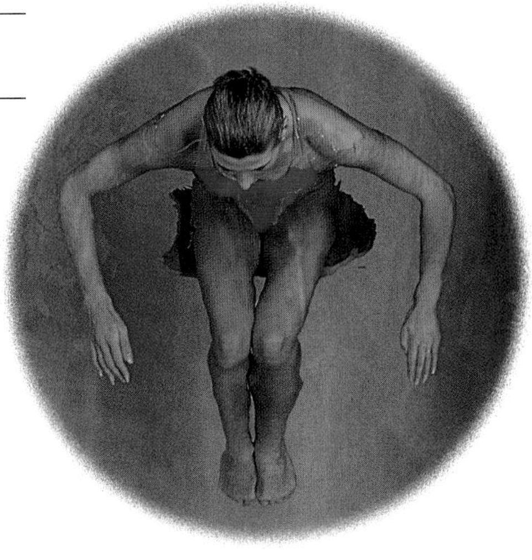

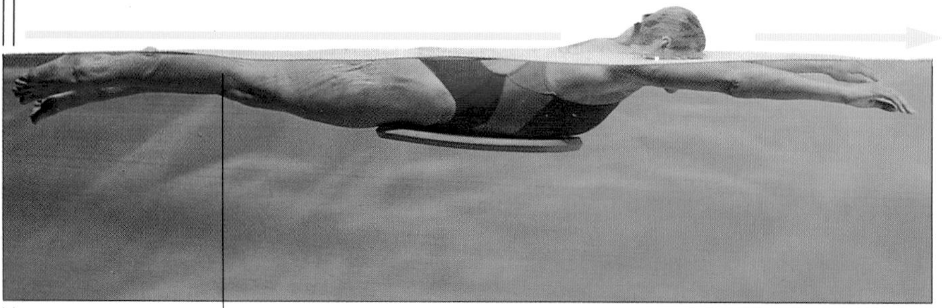

• **CLASSIC POSTURE**
You should feel like an arrow – totally streamlined in the water. Take it calmly – you can always stand on the bottom if necessary.

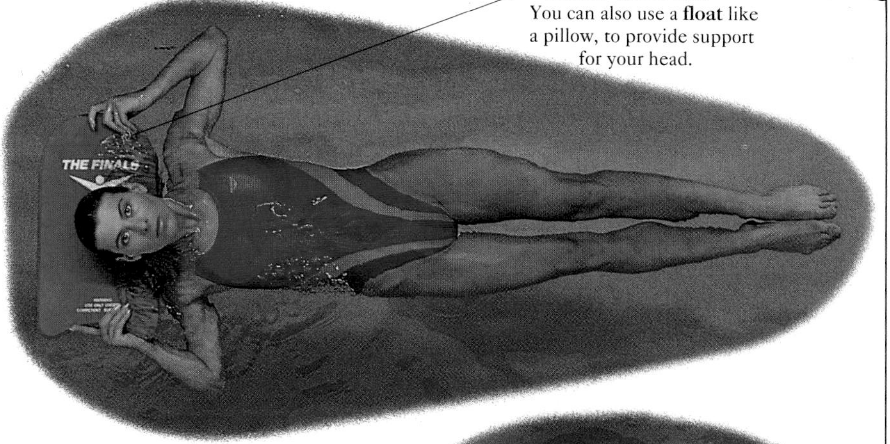

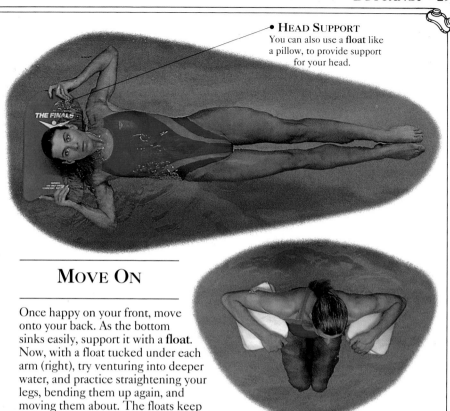

HEAD SUPPORT
You can also use a **float** like a pillow, to provide support for your head.

MOVE ON

Once happy on your front, move onto your back. As the bottom sinks easily, support it with a **float**. Now, with a float tucked under each arm (right), try venturing into deeper water, and practice straightening your legs, bending them up again, and moving them about. The floats keep your upper body well above water.

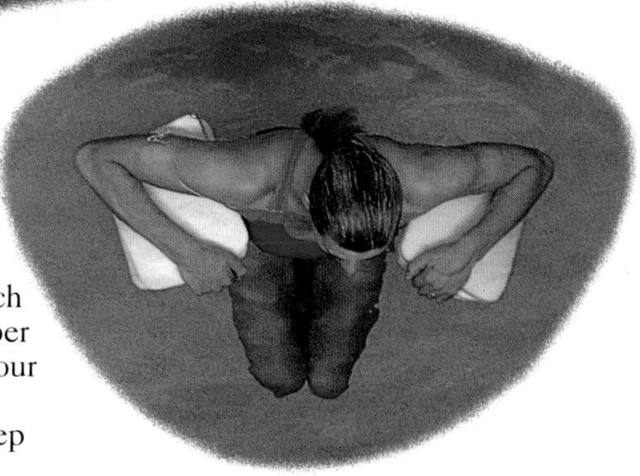

TEST YOUR BUOYANCY

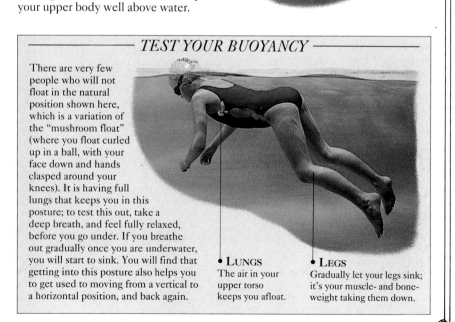

There are very few people who will not float in the natural position shown here, which is a variation of the "mushroom float" (where you float curled up in a ball, with your face down and hands clasped around your knees). It is having full lungs that keeps you in this posture; to test this out, take a deep breath, and feel fully relaxed, before you go under. If you breathe out gradually once you are underwater, you will start to sink. You will find that getting into this posture also helps you to get used to moving from a vertical to a horizontal position, and back again.

LUNGS
The air in your upper torso keeps you afloat.

LEGS
Gradually let your legs sink; it's your muscle- and bone-weight taking them down.

SKILL

3 LEARNING TO MOVE

DAY 1

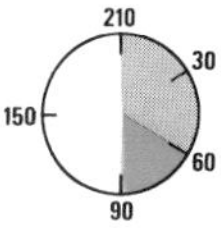

Definition: *Moving, with style, in a streamlined position*

SWIMMING IS A SCIENCE as well as a sport, and to move through water efficiently, you have to keep two main things in mind: first, keep your body horizontal to the surface to reduce water **resistance**; and, second, pull water from in front of you and push it behind you (don't pull it from one side, or from above or below you).

Think of your legs as a boat's engine: speedboats always "hydroplane" (rise up high in the water), because of the powerful engine at the back. We cannot really hydroplane, because we cannot go fast enough naturally, but, by working our legs hard, we can keep as high and horizontal a position as possible. You will use your buttock and thigh muscles for leg propulsion; this takes up quite a lot of energy, and you will find yourself getting tired – this is where doing the exercises on pp.18-19 will help.

OBJECTIVE: To learn how your body moves through water. *Rating* •••

PUSH AND GLIDE

MOVING UNDER THE WATER

To get used to moving and exhaling under the water: put on **flippers**, for extra power, take a deep breath and push yourself off from the poolside, under the surface.

• When the push's momentum fades, make a dolphin-like **undulating** movement with your whole body to move forwards.

• With your head down, arms out, and hands touching, create an arrow shape. This, along with the extra power that the flippers give your legs, helps push you through the water. Breathe out slowly (note the air bubbles). Try doing this across the width of the pool.

SCULLING

Synchronized swimmers owe much of their technique to **sculling**, a skill that gives you a "feel" for water. It is all about finding **new water**, and pushing it from left to right and downwards, which keeps you up in the water. Try it first with **floats** (see pp.28-29), then without, using your wrists and the power in your forearms to push the water. While sculling with your hands, try sculling gently with your legs, using either a breaststroke leg stroke, or a simple "pedaling" action (see below).

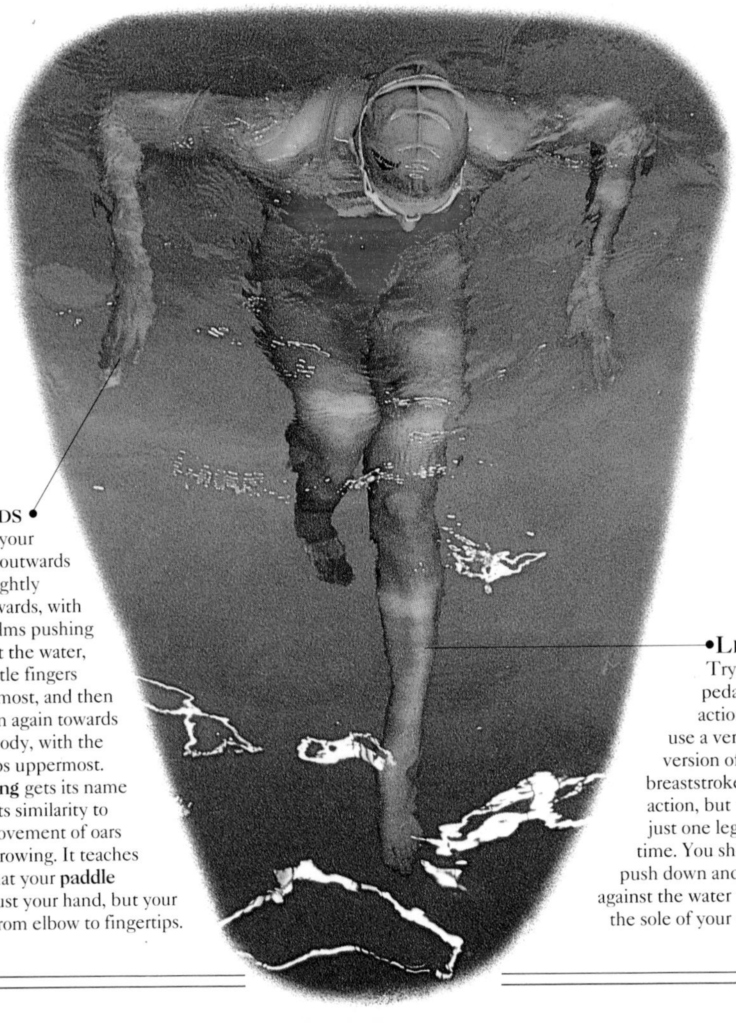

HANDS • Move your hands outwards and slightly downwards, with the palms pushing against the water, and little fingers uppermost, and then back in again towards your body, with the thumbs uppermost. **Sculling** gets its name from its similarity to the movement of oars when rowing. It teaches you that your **paddle** isn't just your hand, but your arm, from elbow to fingertips.

• **LEGS** Try this pedaling action, or use a vertical version of the breaststroke leg action, but with just one leg at a time. You should push down and out against the water with the sole of your foot.

SKILL 3

RESISTANCE

Think of water as a solid object. To test how **resistant** water can be (to your body's **density**), try these **drills**:

1. Float on edge
Stand about chest deep in water and lean forwards slightly. Hold a **float** out in front of you, underneath and edge on to the water; walk forwards slowly. Feel the resistance of the water.

2. Float square-on
Now try repeating Step 1, but hold the float so that it is square-on to the water. Notice how the task of moving forwards has become that much harder compared to Step 1.

If you imagine that the float is your body, these two exercises show you that if your body is at an angle, and positioned down in the water, it is harder to move forwards than if it is in a streamlined, horizontal position, up near the water's surface.

1. ON EDGE

2. SQUARE-ON

HELP FROM AIDS

Following on from the basic pushing and **gliding** exercise on p.30, try some further work on your leg actions. Kicking gives you propulsion, and keeps your lower body, which tends to sink, in a horizontal position. Practice kicking with the use of **kickboards** and **flippers**; such **aids** help you to concentrate on the leg action and "rev up" your engine (your legs) – and they make the actions easier. Holding on to a kickboard, and wearing flippers, try kicking from the hips, down through well-stretched legs. Your knees bend slightly, but point your toes and kick as near the surface as possible. As one leg drives down, the other comes up, and so on, alternately. If you aren't a total novice, you can now try practicing the arm action of any stroke by putting a **pull-buoy** between your legs.

1. When practicing any kind of leg action by holding a **kickboard**, look straight ahead, and keep your body in a streamlined position.

2. Using a **pull-buoy** keeps your legs afloat and up in the water while you concentrate on practicing arm actions.

MOVING FORWARD

LEG POWER

Look at this speedboat, and then look at the shot of the butterfly stroke below. The movement of the water by the swimmer's legs shows the force of the leg kick. The boat and the swimmer have risen up, thrusting through the water. These images illustrate how your legs are your "engine". Remember, you only move forwards if you move water; kicking air gets you nowhere. Always keep as much of your leg-work (and your arm-work) in the water as possible.

Leg propulsion

WATERFLOW

This breaststroke picture (right) shows the direction in which your arms must move the water, from in front of you to behind you, so that you move forward. In the overhead view below, see how the water is still moving backwards from the previous backsweep of the arms. Once you've got a piece of water moving, you must find **new water,** a "wall" to push backwards in order to keep moving forward. Because you lose momentum if you push against water that is already moving, try to make arches or keyhole shapes with your arms (see pp.48, 64), rather than moving them in straight lines.

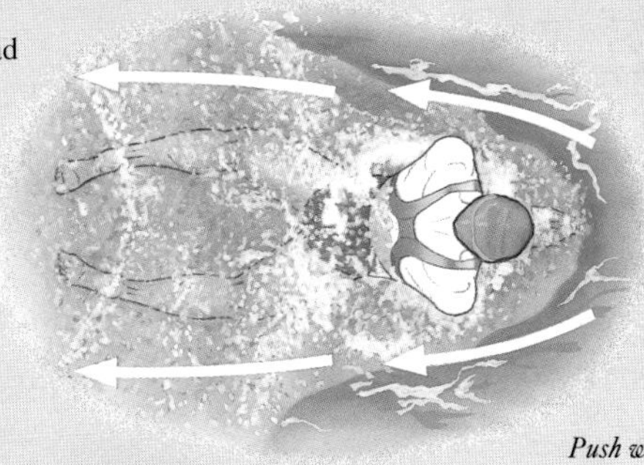

Push water behind you to move forward

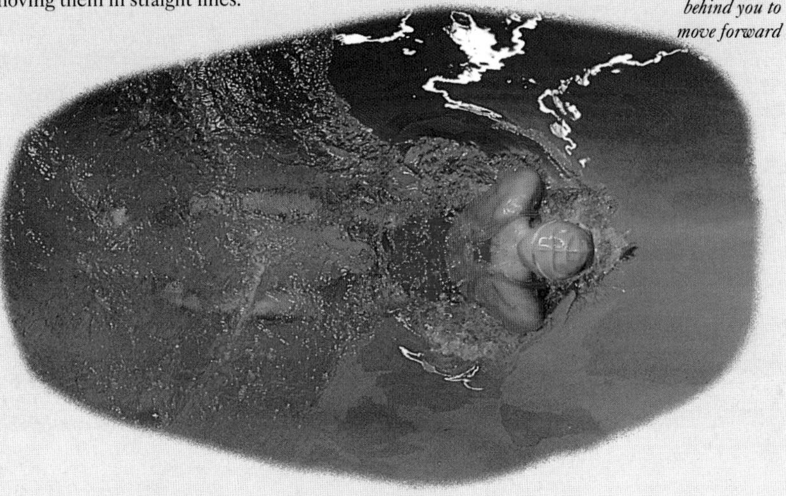

SKILL

DAY 1

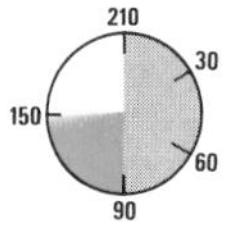

4 BREASTSTROKE

Definition: *Symmetrical arm and leg movements, with the body pivoting on the breast*

MANY SWIMMERS learn breaststroke first, and continue it as a leisurely, recreational stroke: it is the slowest stroke because little or none of the **recovery** (the final stage of an arm or leg action) occurs above water. However, it is actually the most technically demanding stroke to master properly – as it revolves around good timing, and requires excellent co-ordination.

OBJECTIVE: To make symmetrical, co-ordinated strokes quickly and correctly. *Rating* •••••

LEG ACTION

Step 1

FULL STRETCH

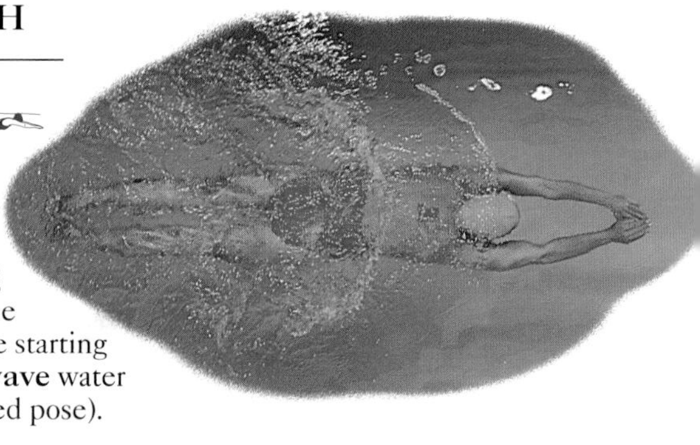

Stretch your legs out, and extend your arms (right), ready to start **catching** (parting) the water and **pulling** back (below). Beginners: try the **glide** shown on the right before starting the sequence (note the **bow wave** water effect caused by the streamlined pose).

• FEET
The legs are fully extended, while the feet are still slightly **flexed** (bent) from the end of the last backwards kick (see p.37).

HEAD •
Your head must be down in the water to keep you streamlined. This is the lowest your head should go.

Step 2

INTO THE BEND

Start to bend your legs at the knee. Always move both legs together (and both arms together) throughout breaststroke – the view on the right shows the kind of symmetry you should be aiming for. At this stage, your arms are completing their "propulsive" phase (propelling you forwards).

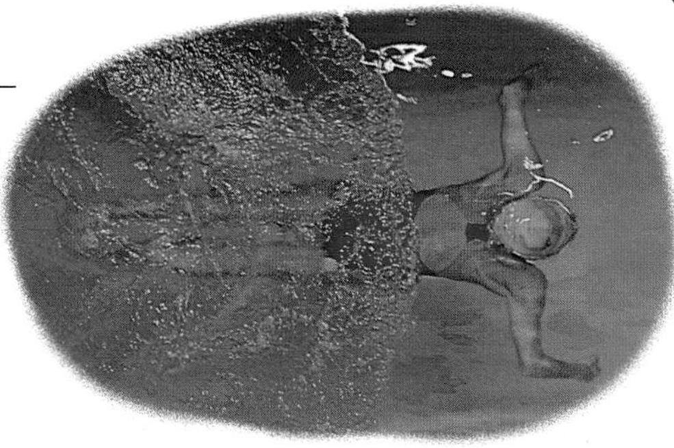

KEEP YOUR KNEES TOGETHER
Your knees should be as close together as possible, making you a narrow and streamlined shape.

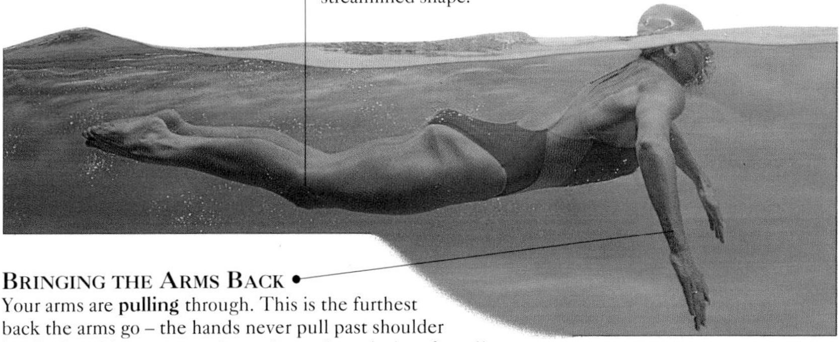

BRINGING THE ARMS BACK
Your arms are **pulling** through. This is the furthest back the arms go – the hands never pull past shoulder level; after this your arms thrust forwards again (see Step 3).

SWIMMING FOR SYMMETRY

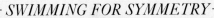

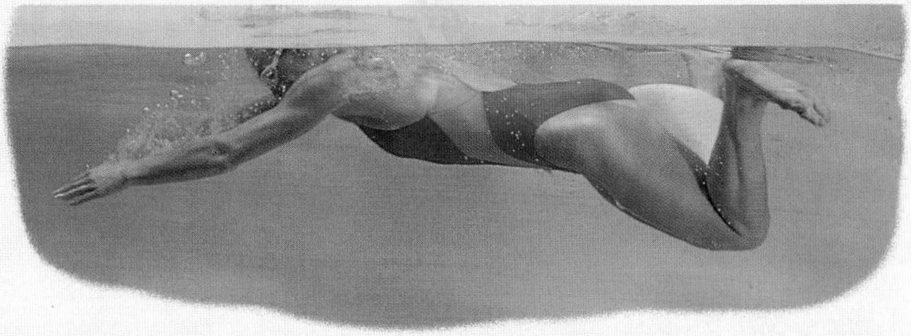

NARROW KNEE APPROACH

Breaststroke should be symmetrical and synchronized, but many swimmers have a **screw kick**. This is where one leg does something slightly different to the other when you kick backwards (see p.37). To get into the habit of keeping both knees aligned during the kick (see above), try placing a **float** between your legs as shown. You will find it difficult to kick using the float, because you can only use the bottom half of your legs, which reduces the degree of propulsion. However, this **drill** does help to prevent screw kicking.

SKILL 4

Step 3

MAKING A RECOVERY

Bend your legs further at the knees, and bring your feet up. Keep your heels as close together as possible, but avoid letting them touch. Your feet should stay **flexed** backwards and outwards. This stage heralds the start of the **recovery** stage for the legs – the phase that will, ultimately, return the legs to their original extended position. Your arms are also going into recovery; they have completed their **pulling** movement as you bring them back in towards your body and forwards (see also the overhead photograph at the bottom of the page). This arm action will automatically lift your upper body out of the water – providing you with the perfect opportunity to take a breath.

TAKING A BREATHER
Your head lifts out of the water at this stage, so take a breath before stretching forwards again. Inhale on every stroke, not every second or third stroke.

HEELS
As your knees begin to bend and part slightly, your heels should be about hip-width apart.

SQUEEZING AND SCULLING
While your arms are coming inwards as you squeeze your elbows together, your hands perform a **sculling** type of action – the palms go from facing slightly out, with the fingers down, to facing each other, with your fingers pointing forwards (see p.31).

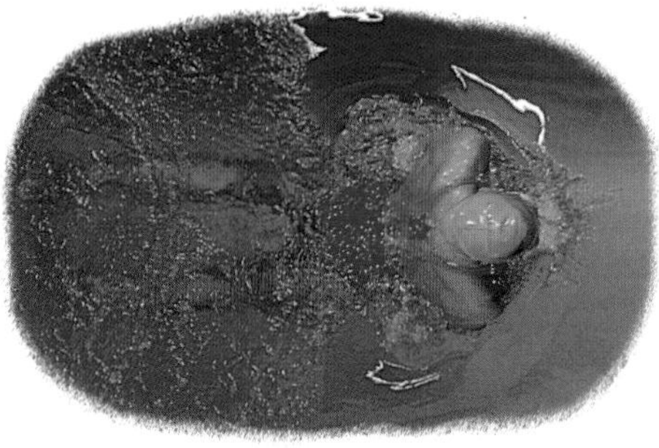

FROM THE TOP
The overhead photograph (left) shows clearly how the legs have parted and the arms have come back into the body and forwards, having completed their **pull** through the water. You can see that the elbows are tucked in close and the fingers are pointing forwards, palms together, ready for their next extension and outward sweep.

Step 4

THE LEG KICK

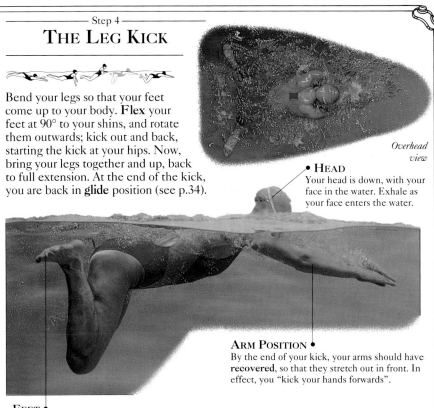

Bend your legs so that your feet come up to your body. **Flex** your feet at 90° to your shins, and rotate them outwards; kick out and back, starting the kick at your hips. Now, bring your legs together and up, back to full extension. At the end of the kick, you are back in **glide** position (see p.34).

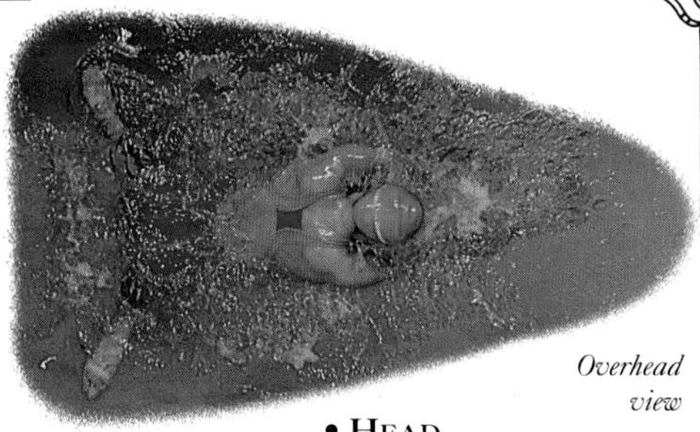

Overhead view

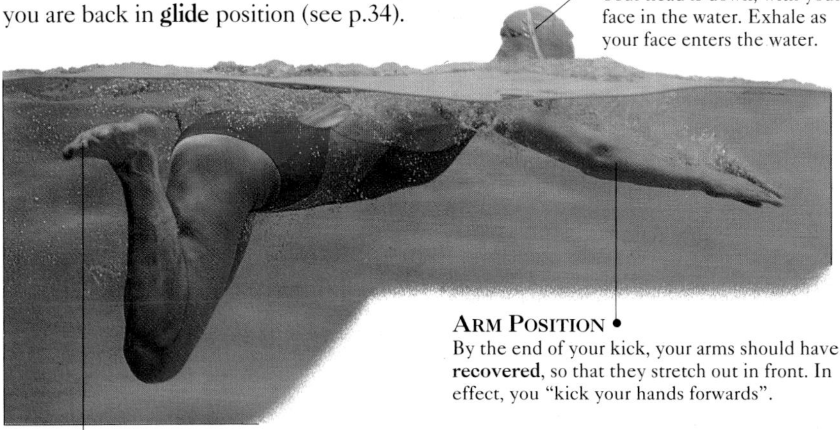

HEAD
Your head is down, with your face in the water. Exhale as your face enters the water.

ARM POSITION
By the end of your kick, your arms should have **recovered**, so that they stretch out in front. In effect, you "kick your hands forwards".

FEET
Your **flexed** feet, with toes pulled back towards your shins, create **paddles** that push against the water, providing strong backward thrust. Feel the flexion right through to your hips.

THE KICK
The accepted style for the kick used to be stiff, but is now a more fluent **whip kick**, where feet and ankles come up together before parting, pushing back, and coming together again.

LEG ACTION CHECKLIST

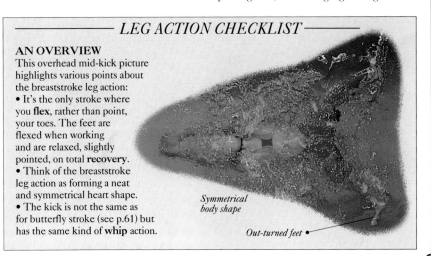

AN OVERVIEW
This overhead mid-kick picture highlights various points about the breaststroke leg action:
• It's the only stroke where you **flex**, rather than point, your toes. The feet are flexed when working and are relaxed, slightly pointed, on total **recovery**.
• Think of the breaststroke leg action as forming a neat and symmetrical heart shape.
• The kick is not the same as for butterfly stroke (see p.61) but has the same kind of **whip** action.

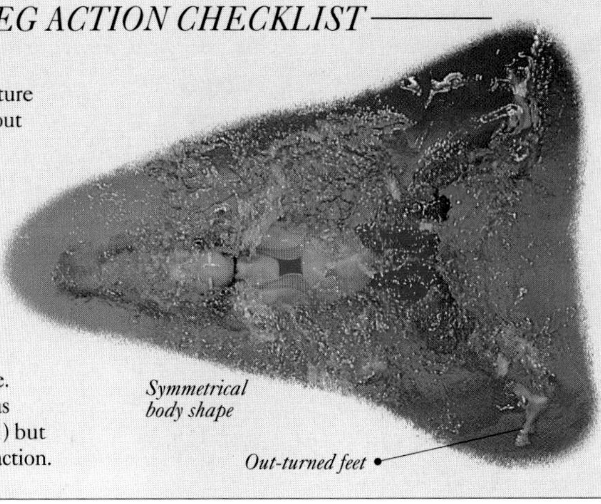

Symmetrical body shape

Out-turned feet

SKILL 4

ARM ACTION

Step 1

THE CATCH

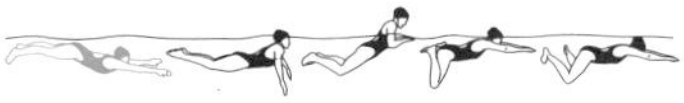

You've completed the kick; your legs have come together again, and are extended. Your arms are also stretched out, in front of you. Now, start to **catch** hold of the water with your hands and arms, **pulling** your arms diagonally down and out. Look forwards, to see where you're going, not at the pool bottom.

BOTTOM UP
Having successfully completed the kick, your bottom should be back up in the water.

ARMS AND HANDS – PARTING THE WATER
Don't bend your arms yet; this puts the brakes on. Use the propulsion from the kick. Make sure that you keep your arms just under the water, and angle your palms out, with your little finger uppermost.

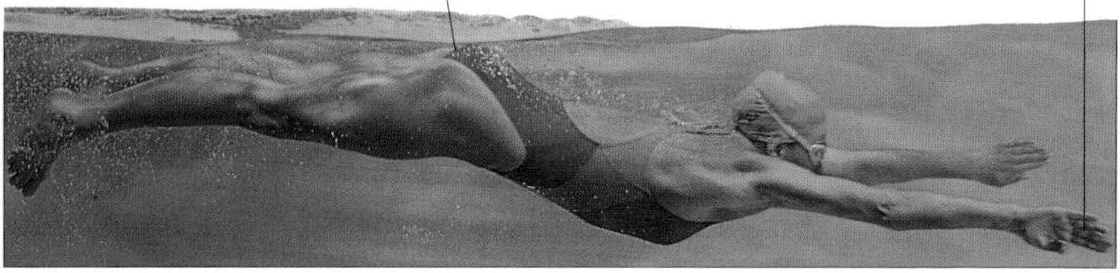

USING THE LEG KICK
The powerful backward leg kick will propel you forward – make use of this propulsion to **glide** a little way.

DIVE POSITION

STRAIGHT AS AN ARROW
For competitive swimmers, this full-stretch **glide** pose, at the start of the sequence, is only a split-second rest phase, with no propulsive arm or leg action. Think of it as a straight dive into water; then imagine a line drawn through the middle of the body, so that one half mirrors the other.

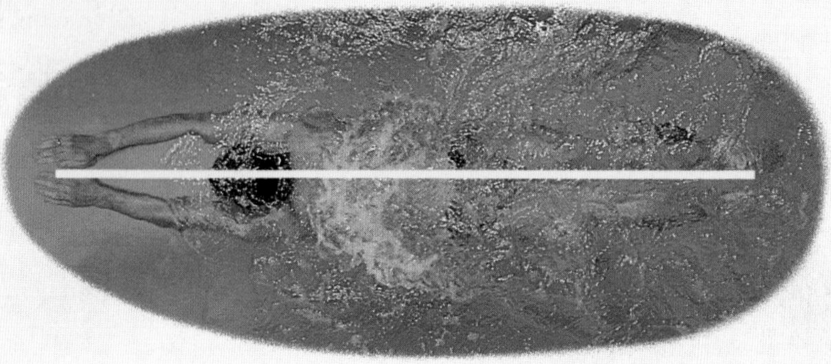

GAINING HEIGHT

SQUEEZE PRACTICE
Gain the height needed to practice the arm "squeeze" by doing the butterfly leg kick with **flippers** on. You can't do breaststroke kick wearing flippers, because you can't **flex** your feet. Try to squirt water out in front as your arms move together and up.

Step 2

FULL ARM PULL

Bring your arms down – your hands **pull** sideways, downwards, and backwards, with fingers slightly open as you get hold of the water. At the deepest point of the move, the lower arms are at 90° to the body, the upper arms level with the shoulders, and bent elbows high. Your hands don't go back past shoulder level.

Step 3

THE SQUEEZE

Squeeze your elbows together, into your body, bringing yourself up to full height and taking a breath. Your arms don't provide propulsion at this stage, so your palms can be together or crossed (for a streamlined kind of shape).

GET YOURSELF READY
You're about to stretch your arms forwards (helped by the leg kick).

EXHALING
The bubbles show that you have nearly finished exhaling.

PADDLES
Make the most of your **paddles**, which are from your fingers to your elbows; don't just use your hands. Hands should be kept **soft**, not stiff.

SKILL
4

Step 4

STRETCHING OUT

As your heels come up together towards your bottom, ready to kick out backwards, start to stretch your arms right out in front of you. At this point, your head should be half in, half out, of the water, and you should just have taken a full breath in. Keep your arms fully extended – the bubbles in the photograph below give some indication of the force of the forward stretch.

ONWARDS AND FORWARDS
Your hands are **pushing** forwards. As long as your palms are fairly close together, to reduce water **resistance**, it doesn't matter whether they face down or are together.

"HEELS TO BOTTOM"
Make sure that you keep your heels right up, as close to your bottom as possible.

ARM POSITION
Remember, straight arms will make your body more streamlined.

KNEES
Keep your knees bent, behind and below your hips, and keep your hips as high as possible – in order to reduce water **resistance**.

STAY STREAMLINED

LOW RESISTANCE
As you extend your arms forwards, keep them just below the surface, and your head down, so that your body forms as streamlined a shape as possible, from fingertips to buttocks. This pose, and keeping the hands close together as you **push** forwards, reduces water **resistance**. Ensure that water resistance is kept to a minimum – if it is not, you will find that breaststroke can all too easily become jerky, going from fast to slow and then fast again.

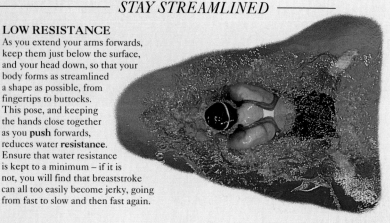

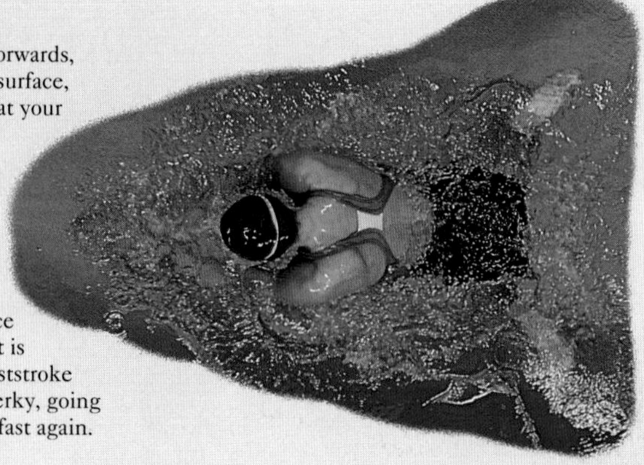

SYMMETRY IN ACTION

MIRROR-IMAGE ACTIONS
Viewed head-on and feet-on, imagine a vertical line running down the center of a swimmer as he or she does breaststroke. Note the symmetry in the arm actions, and in the leg actions. Below, you can see the main stages of the breaststroke arm and leg sequences. Remember that the main stages of the leg action don't coincide with those of the arm action (their arrangement here, under each other, is not meant to indicate that they coincide).

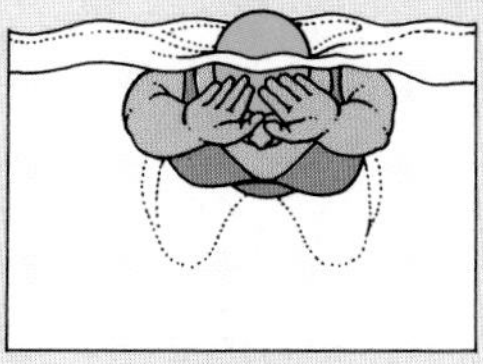

1.Full-stretch, face down

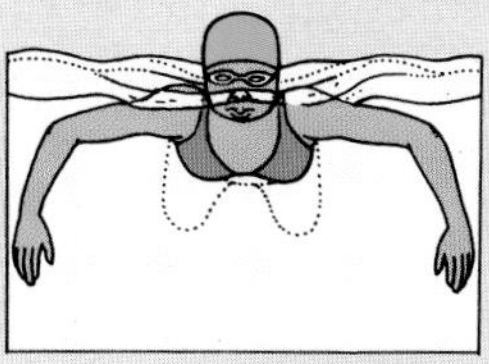

*2.**Pulling** back; high elbows*

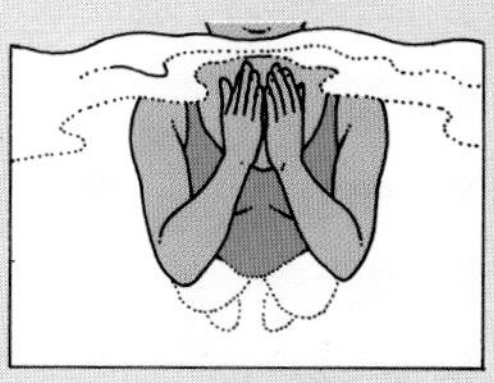

*3.Hands drawn up for **recovery***

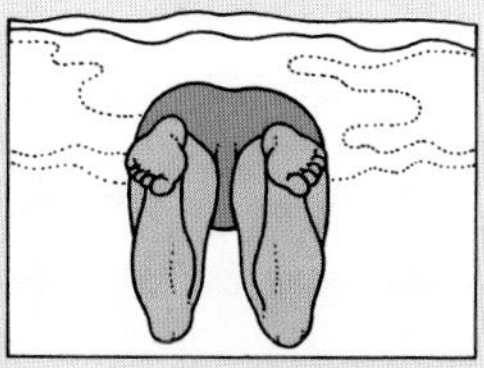

1.Legs cocked, ready to kick

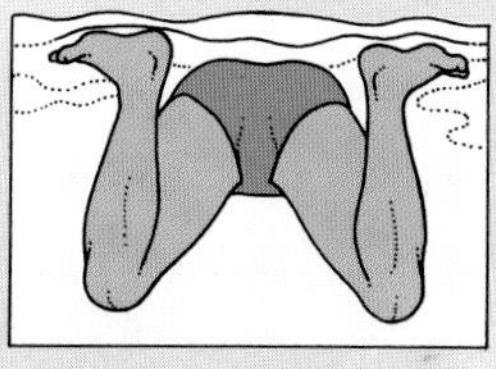

*2.Backwards kick, **flexed** feet*

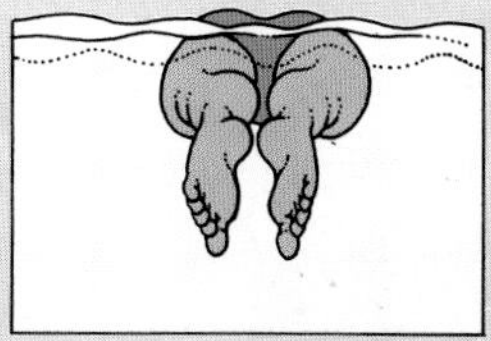

3.Back together, at full extension

Step 5

TOWARDS COMPLETION

As you kick your legs back vigorously (notice the bubbles around the feet), keep your head low and your arms streamlined. Try to get your arms as close to the water's surface as you can, as you **recover** to a stretched-out pose.

• **LEGS**
Whether doing a **whip kick**, or a wider **wedge**-shaped kick, kick with both legs at the same time; avoid a **screw kick**. Make your strokes rhythmical, strong, and fluid; **undulate** through the water.

CHECK ARM HEIGHT •
As you complete the kick, your arms should, preferably, be even higher in the water, and more streamlined, than shown here.

SKILL

4

STARTING TO CATCH THE WATER
Your hands move out and down, palms outwards, as they begin to **catch** the water.

BEND AND PULL
Your legs begin to bend, as your arms reach the deepest point of the **pull**.

IN SEQUENCE

This full sequence shows clearly how your arms and legs should be working in order to produce a fluid style, and to keep up the kind of momentum seen in butterfly stroke. Always keep in your mind the special interaction between the arms and legs: when the arms work, the legs **recover**; when the legs work, the arms recover – the arms and legs working constantly in time to propel you forwards. There is little activity above water (except breathing and squeezing the arms together), so your actions must be correct, to counter water **resistance**.

LEG ACTION
The leg action is a push-**recover**, push-recover movement, rather than the "engine" effect of other strokes, where your pointed feet work more like a motor. Timing is critical: push with your feet, then **pull** with your arms.

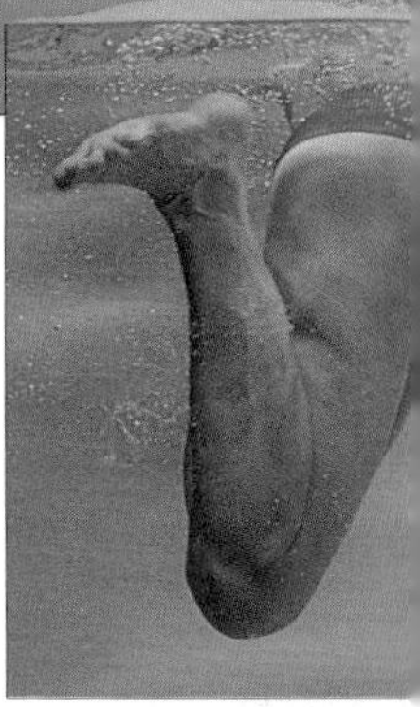

DRILLS FOR BREASTSTROKE SKILLS

KICK BACK

Practice putting your hands by your bottom and doing leg kicks, trying each time to touch fingers-to-heels (below). This **drill** teaches you to bring your feet right up to your body in a synchronized motion.

HEAD DOWN

Swim a few lengths while concentrating on keeping a low head. Novices may like to hold their faces up in the air; but you need a low head to gain speed (to overcome water **resistance**), and to get a good rhythm.

• FULL SQUEEZE
Tuck your elbows in, hard to your sides; if you squirt water out in front, you've got a good, strong action.

BREASTSTROKE POINTERS

Follow Steps 1-5 and try for a fluid stroke. The more leisurely your approach, the more you may wish to **glide**. Keep your hips and bottom up. Your head should ideally be down a little in the full-stretch phase, keeping you streamlined. Your hands **catch** the water and start to **pull** down and out, with **soft** fingers – slightly open and relaxed (Steps 1&2). Your hands come together quickly under your chest, in a squeeze that creates its own wave (Step 3). Your feet **flex** back, ready to spring into the kick. Reach forwards with your arms as your face enters the water (Step 4). After pushing back through your feet (Step 5), you will be back in the **glide** phase.

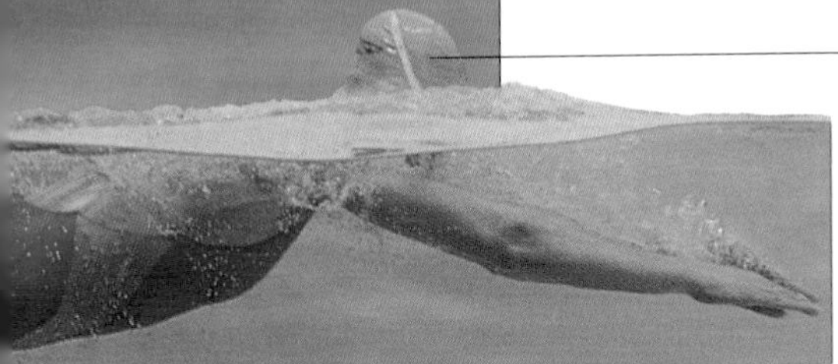

• HEAD DOWN
Your head goes back down, and your feet should be right up, ready to kick.

COMPLETION •
Your arms stretch out. Your **flexed** feet kick back, pushing against the water, ready to **glide** a little and start the stroke again.

SKILL

DAY 1

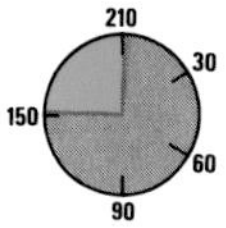

5 BACKSTROKE

Definition: *A variation of the front crawl, performed on your back*

THE **BACKSTROKE** is the third fastest stroke. It is the only stroke where your face never has to enter the water (although you inevitably get water on your face), so the timing of the breathing is not as critical as for the other strokes. Because of this, it can be a good first stroke to learn – provided you are comfortable with not being able to see where you are going.

OBJECTIVE: To propel yourself forwards, while lying on your back, in as straight a line as possible. *Rating* ••••

FLOAT PRACTICE

Before trying the full stroke, beginners might like to practice floating on their backs with a **float** under the head, like a pillow. Practice this until you feel confident in the **backstroke** position. This practice pose is comfortable for breathing, and helps you to keep your body high and horizontal in the water.

FLAT OUT
This **drill** helps you stay horizontal, counteracting the legs' natural tendency to sink when the body is in the **backstroke** position. If possible, try to be even higher and flatter than shown below.

USING A FLOAT
As well as giving support, the **float** encourages you to tuck your chin into your chest slightly, giving you the correct, aerodynamic head position for the **backstroke**.

GET IT STRAIGHT
This **backstroke** picture (right) shows the straight, close-to-the-surface position that you should aim for – the same principle as for the front crawl, but on your back.

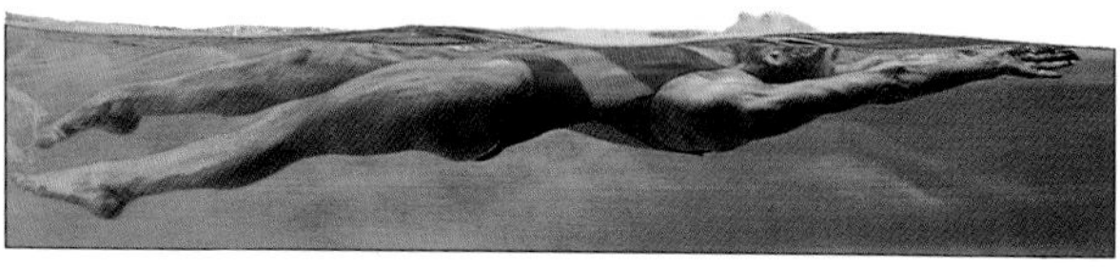

FLIPPERS FOR FLEXIBILITY

PADDLE POWER
Wearing **flippers** lets you feel how flexible the ankles and toes should be for the **backstroke** kick. They also help you develop a deep kick and keep it underwater – vital for good propulsion. Your feet should only break the surface slightly, and gently, if at all. A strong kick doesn't mean making lots of splash; in fact, splashing usually means that you're simply kicking air, which gives no thrust at all. Your legs must bend at the knee in order to kick, but avoid "pedaling", which wastes energy. Flippers help your legs stay as straight as possible, although they should be **soft** – relaxed, not stiffly straight.

KICK PRACTICE

Now perfect a good body position while practicing the **backstroke** kick. With **flippers** on, and arms above your head, drive one leg down as the other comes up (see box above). The kick is similar to the front crawl – kick from the hip and thigh muscles. Feel your body rolling on a line that runs from between your hands down to your flippers. The key to good backstroke is not to swim flat on your back, but to roll from side to side with each alternate stroke, in a rocking motion.

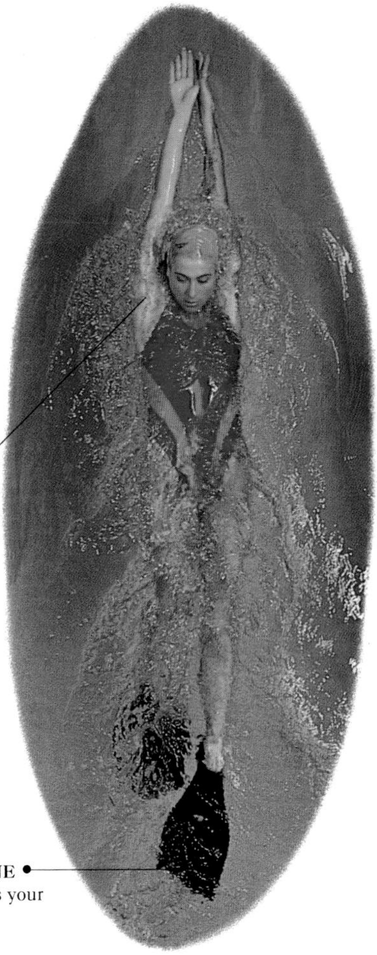

ARMS AND HANDS
Keep your arms outstretched and your palms open, with thumbs touching or on top of each other (cross your wrists or clasp your hands if you wish). This produces an arrow shape that helps to propel you, like a boat's bow, through the water. If you put your arms by your side, your shoulders create a breakwater that impedes progress.

LOOK IN THE RIGHT DIRECTION
Novices often feel uneasy about the backstroke because they can't see where they're going. Instead of looking at the ceiling, which puts your head in the wrong position, pick a point on the wall that you're swimming away from, and keep looking at that to stay on-course.

REVVING THE ENGINE
Wearing **flippers** upgrades your "engine" (your legs).

SKILL 5

LEG ACTION

KEEP KICKING

The **backstroke** leg action is a continuous up-and-down drive with alternate legs: the kick you started learning on page 45. Practice until you feel confident; don't add the arm action yet. Once you've mastered this kick, you're well on the way to a good backstroke. Keep your legs kicking up and down in a long, relatively straight action coming from the hips, bottom, and thighs – not the knees.

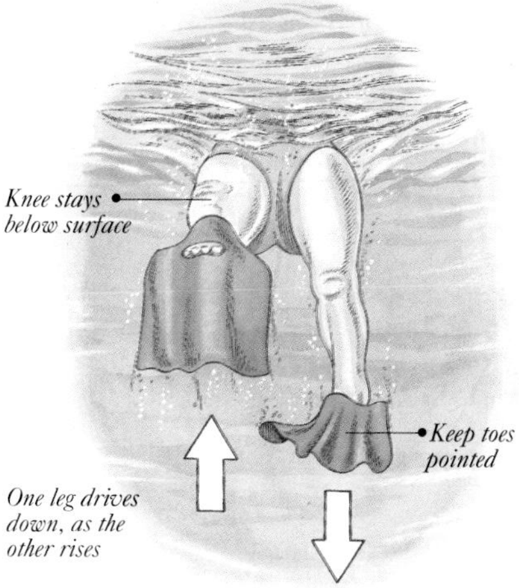
Knee stays below surface
Keep toes pointed
One leg drives down, as the other rises

UP AND DOWN

Above: On the up-kick, stretch your ankles and toes in a vigorous upwards action. On the down-kick, keep your leg as straight as you can and drive from your bottom and thighs. **Flippers** help stop your knees from breaking the surface.

INCORRECT • Here, the knee is bent too far – don't bend it more than 45°. If you do, you are simply kicking the water up and down, which doesn't give good propulsion.

CORRECT • Keep the legs relatively straight. Your feet "churn", not break, the surface.

Keep your arms above your head, hands together, as on p.45.

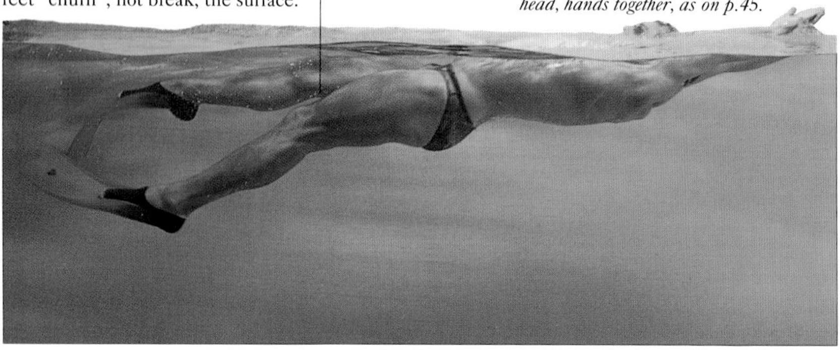

ARM ACTION

Step 2

LITTLE FINGER FIRST

You've brought one hand out of the water, little finger first, as the other entered, little finger first. Keep the kick going. The picture below shows your position just after the blue figure above.

LEADING THE WAY
Above: The little finger leads the hand out of the water.

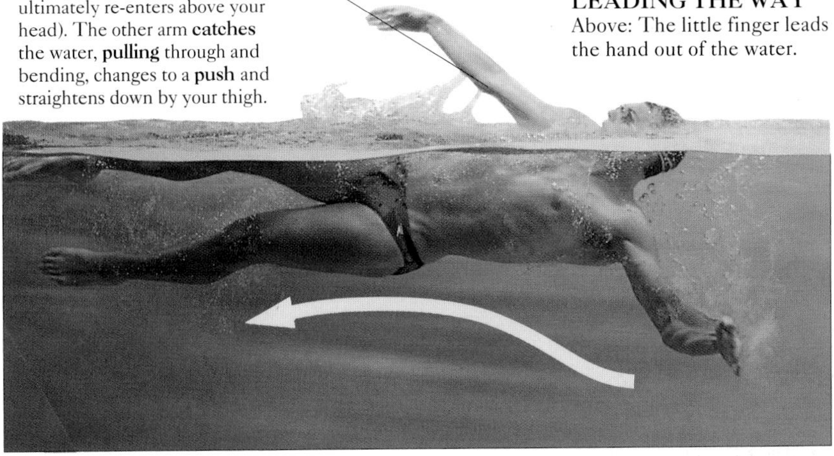

UP AND OVER •
This arm comes up, straight (it ultimately re-enters above your head). The other arm **catches** the water, **pulling** through and bending, changes to a **push** and straightens down by your thigh.

ALTERNATING BODY ROLL
As your left hand enters the water, let your body roll to the left, and vice versa; don't stiffen. This roll gives you depth, ensuring that your arms have as much water to **pull** and **push** as possible.

KEEP IT LIGHT
As your arm starts to **pull** down and sideways through the water (above), keep your fingers **light** – that is, neither stiff and squeezed together, nor wide open.

CATCHING THE WATER
As your right hand enters the water, with the little finger leading, start to find **new water** (see p.33), from your right shoulder down, preparing for a fast **push**-through.

SKILL 5

Step 3

PULL-PUSH

Once past shoulder level, your left hand changes its action from a **pull** to a **push**. The harder you push with this hand, the better the entry with your other, **recovering**, hand, which is now at full stretch, above the water. Imagine you're trying to touch the ceiling with your recovering hand, and stretch this arm right up, almost lifting your shoulder into your face.

RECOVERING HAND
Start to rotate your palm outwards, away from your body, ready to re-enter the water, little finger first.

HEAD AND FACE
Look back diagonally at the wall you are leaving, not up at the ceiling. Throughout the stroke, keep your ears submerged, but your face above the water. Take a breath as one arm **recovers**, and exhale as your other arm recovers.

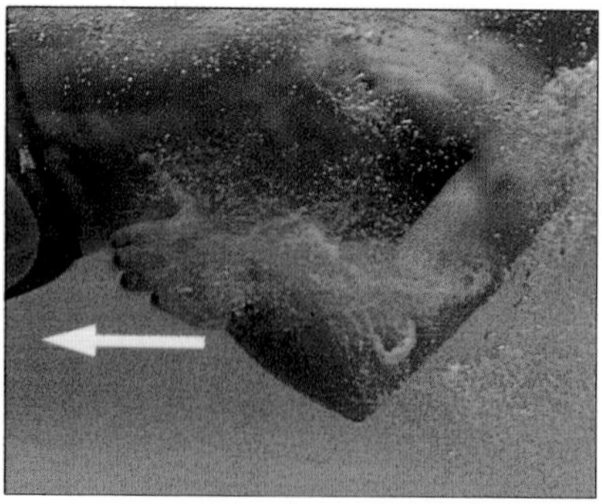

HAND POSITION
Note the right-angled hand position on the downsweeping arm. This angle helps to give the arm power as it finishes **pulling** and goes into the **push** stage.

SHAPING UP

MAKE AN S-SHAPED PATH
An S-shaped downsweep, through different water depths, ensures that the arm keeps finding **new water** to move. If it moved in a straight line, it would meet less **resistance** and give less momentum.

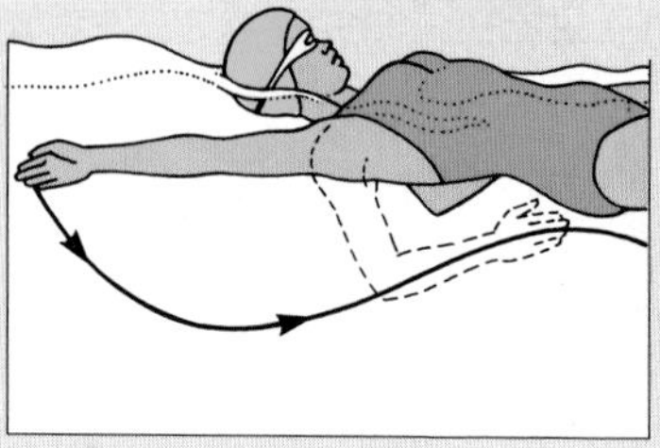

Step 4

STRAIGHTENING OUT

At the end of your left hand's **push** through the water, your left arm straightens so that it comes down and in towards the thigh; don't make it too stiff. A hard down-push helps the entry of the other arm, and a fast entry will create more depth and power at the end of the push, so timing is vital. At the end of the push, your wrist makes a slight "whipping" action (the fingers whip down, rather like a riding crop being cracked). On the shot below (taken just before the blue figure above), note the bubbles produced by the force of the push, and the spurting water by the speed of the **recovering** hand.

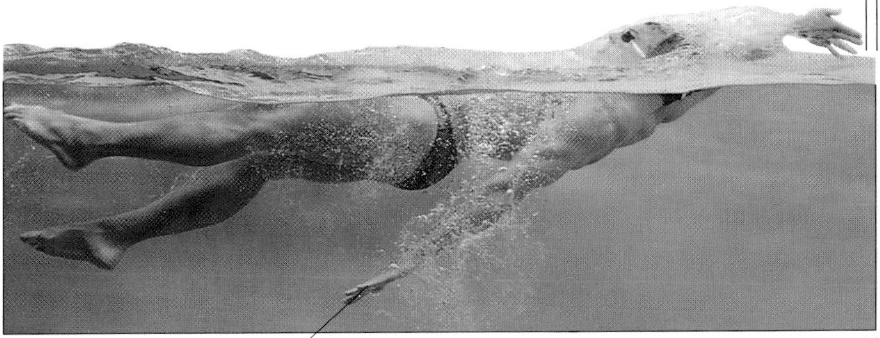

CORRECT PALM POSITION

After the arm has straightened, the hand turns so that the palm is facing backwards; ready for the little finger to exit first.

"ACTION AND REACTION"

Right: Working one arm hard naturally brings the other shoulder up, in a side-to-side roll. Think of this as "lift, roll, press": as one arm rises, the other arm rolls down, its hand pressing the water.

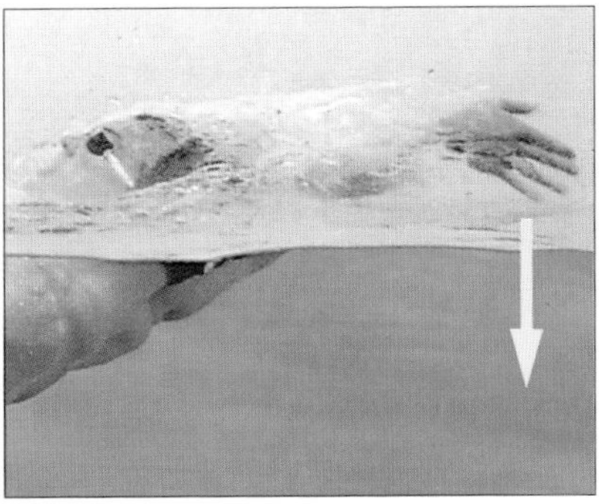

GOING IN

Entry with the side of your hand, little finger first, places your hand in a relatively deep position, which will greatly improve how you **catch** the water.

*The **backstroke** seen from above*

SKILL
5

ON A ROLL
Imagine a bar through the center of the body, creating an axis along which you roll. Lie close to the surface.

ANGLED HEAD
Look up diagonally, at the far wall, not up at the ceiling.

GOOD ENTRY
Entering little finger first positions the hand for a good **catch** and **pull.**

THE KICK
The kick starts from the thigh; don't over-bend your knee. Much of the kick is side on, due to the body's roll.

IN SEQUENCE

This full sequence shows how vital your body's side-to-side roll is in helping your arms – from shoulder to little finger – enter, **pull**, and **push** the body through the water, finding **new water** all the time. Because the **backstroke**, like the front crawl, uses alternate arm movements, you will veer off-course if one arm action is stronger or more streamlined than the other. A common mistake is one arm entering the water at a different distance from the body to the other. Slow your stroke down in order to concentrate on perfecting your style; it is much easier to add speed to a good style than the other way around.

LEGS
Keep your legs going like a motor, holding you high in the water. Keep them as close together and straight as possible; point your toes.

HOW MANY KICKS?
Competitive swimmers do roughly six to eight kicks per arm stroke (more for sprints, and less for distance events).

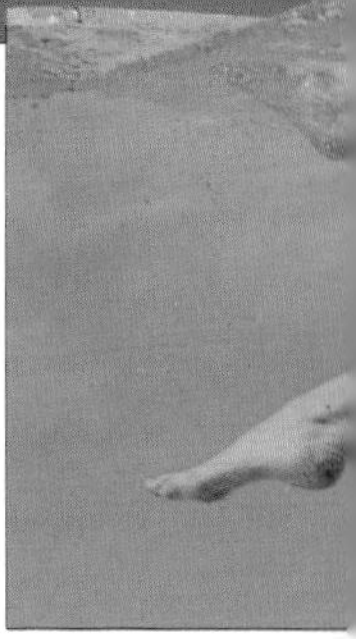

DOUBLE-ARM STYLE

A USEFUL VARIATION

Practicing a simultaneous action with both arms helps you to: 1. Get used to the **back-stroke** position, and a bent elbow **push**. 2. Perfect a straight entry. (Note: you can't roll from side to side when doing this **drill** stroke.)

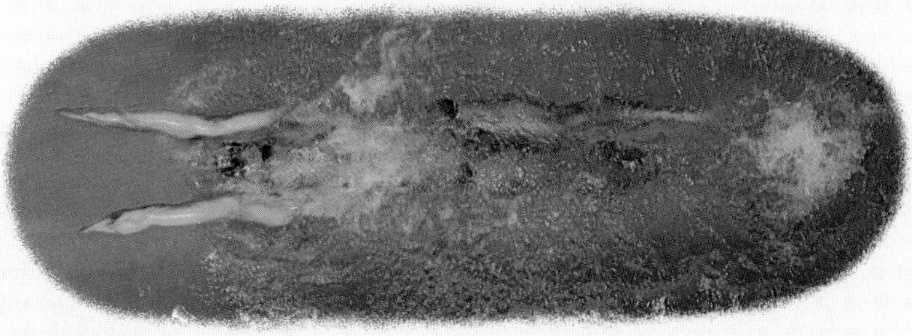

RECOVERY
Now past the shoulder, the hand rotates slightly, ready to enter little finger first.

AGAINST THE CLOCK

Think of your hands' entries in terms of a clock face. Imagine your head at 12 o'clock. One hand should enter the water, little finger first, at 11 o'clock, while the other exits by your thigh and goes up and over, to re-enter at 1 o'clock. Keep hand entry in line with your shoulder, not too far from, or too centered over, your head. A smooth entry (and exit), little finger first, cuts down wasteful splash and water **resistance**.

PULLING THROUGH
The hand **pull-pushes** down and sideways, past the shoulder, and into the body, in an S-shaped path. Remember, pulling in a straight line is like moving your hand in a flowing stream in the same direction as the current: you meet less **resistance** and so get less momentum.

SHOULDER LIFT
The left arm stretches through from the shoulder, which exits first. It is followed by the arm, then the hand, which turns so that the little finger emerges uppermost.

SKILL

6 FRONT CRAWL

DAY 2

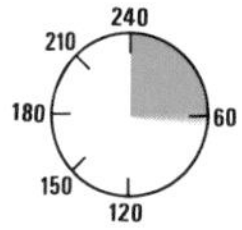

Definition: *An alternating stroke; performed on your front, with your face down in the water*

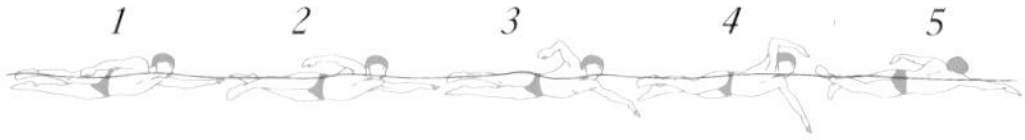

THIS IS THE FASTEST, and probably the most popular, stroke. It is so widely used in competitive **freestyle** races – where the swimmer is free to choose any stroke – that most people now equate freestyle with front crawl. Timing of the breathing, in relation to the arm action, is all-important.

OBJECTIVE: A smooth, fast, and co-ordinated action. *Rating* ••••

LEG ACTION

FLIPPER-WORK

Start off by practicing the leg action without the arm stroke. Hold a **float**, as shown, and wear **flippers**: flippers give extra leg power, and flexibility in your ankles, and promote a good leg motion. The constant up-and-down drive is similar to the **backstroke** kick.

HIPS
Like the **backstroke**, the power in the front crawl kick should come from your hips, bottom, and thighs, not from your knees. Feel your hips and thighs working in a relatively straight, up-and-down action. You will find that wearing **flippers** accentuates the correct muscular movement.

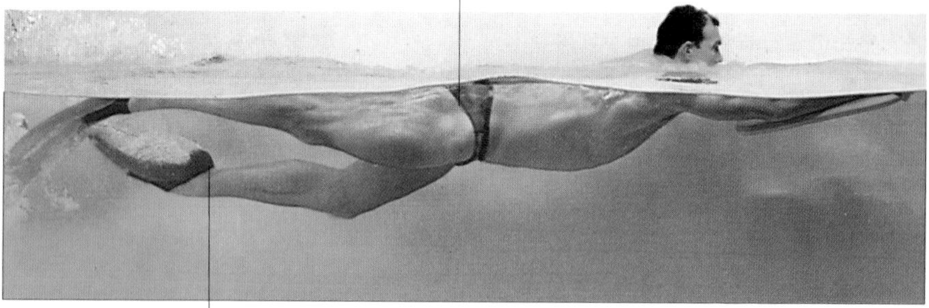

ANKLES
Wearing **flippers** promotes flexible ankles – vital for a streamlined kick action.

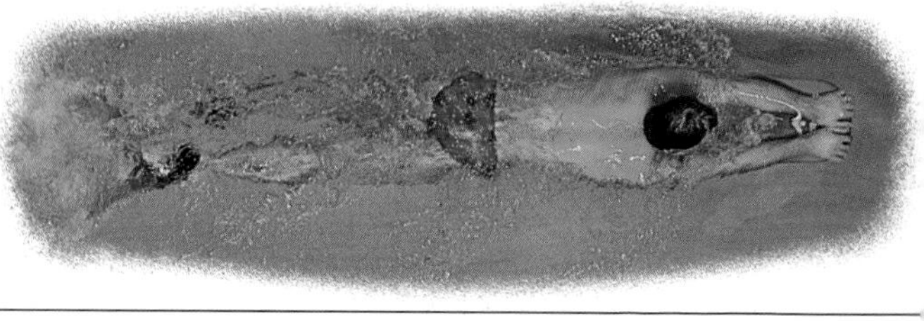

Form a streamlined shape in the water

ON YOUR OWN

Now, try the kick without **flippers** – feel how much more effort you need for the same action. Keep alternate legs going in a continuous kicking motion. Drive your leg down so that your leg is straight at the end of the down-kick, before you drive it up again. Go for depth under the water, not splash above; too much splash means you're kicking air, which gives poor propulsion. Remember: your legs are your "engine", giving more power to your stroke than you may realize.

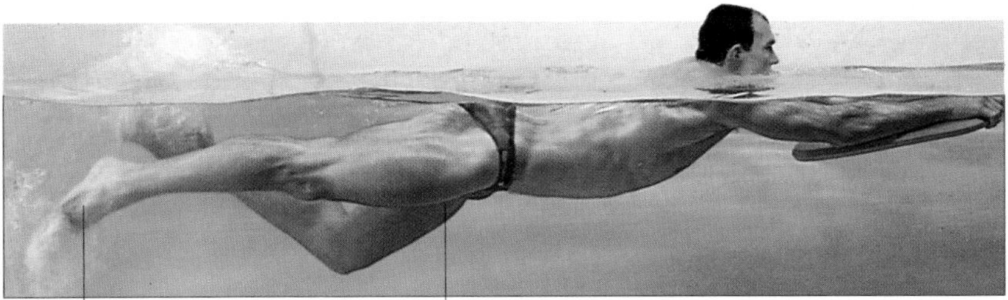

FEET
Your feet should be pointed, and only just breaking the surface. Keep the kick under the water: its propulsive power comes from working against water **resistance**.

LEGS
Notice that the left leg bends more without **flippers**; keep this bend to a minimum. Ensure that your legs are as close together, for a streamlined shape, as possible.

KICKBOARD DRILLS

CONCENTRATING ON KICKS
You will find that using a **kickboard float** means you can perfect the all-important kick before moving on to adding the arm action.

• Using a kickboard float, as shown below, supports your upper body while you concentrate on working your legs.

• Kicking **drills**, with and without **flippers**, and performed holding a float, encourage the streamlined body position necessary for an efficient front crawl – keep in mind that good streamlining means less water **resistance**, and therefore more speed.

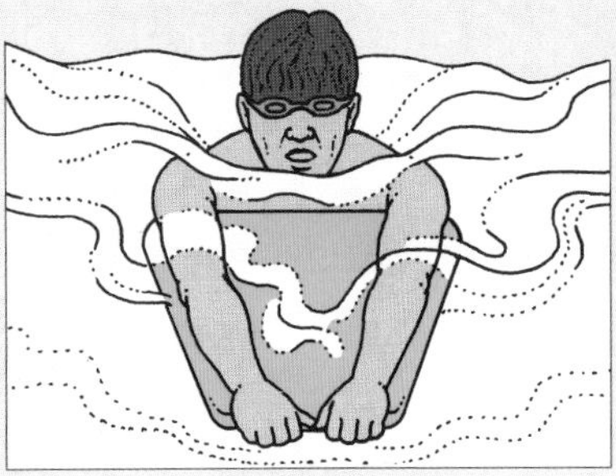

• Even when using a float, keep your head as low as possible. Lifting your head too far up out of the water forces your legs down and your shoulders up, and high shoulders form a breakwater that hampers forward progress.

• Good strong kick-work gives you the freedom to slow your arm stroke down until you get it – and therefore the timing of your breathing – absolutely correct. Over-working your arms is simply wasting energy. Get the legs right first, and the whole stroke will fit together much more easily.

HOLD ON
When using a **kickboard** to practice a leg stroke, hold it over the front with both hands. This puts your body in a balanced, horizontal position, high up in the water.

Skill 6

Arm Action

Step 1

Work and Recovery

While you are maintaining a continuous up-and-down kicking action with alternate legs, your arms should also be alternating – between a working stage and a **recovering** stage. Stretch one arm right out in front of you, while the other reaches your thigh as it finishes **pulling** through. Your front arm starts to sink down, ready to begin **catching** the water. You should be exhaling into the water, in a slow, controlled way, at this stage (see the box, "Getting Your Breathing Right" at the top of p.55).

Coming Out of the Water
This arm has just finished its backwards **push**, and will soon be coming up, out of the water.

Getting Ready for the Catch
The palm of your front hand, facing down at this stage of the arm stroke, will start to face backwards as it **pulls** down.

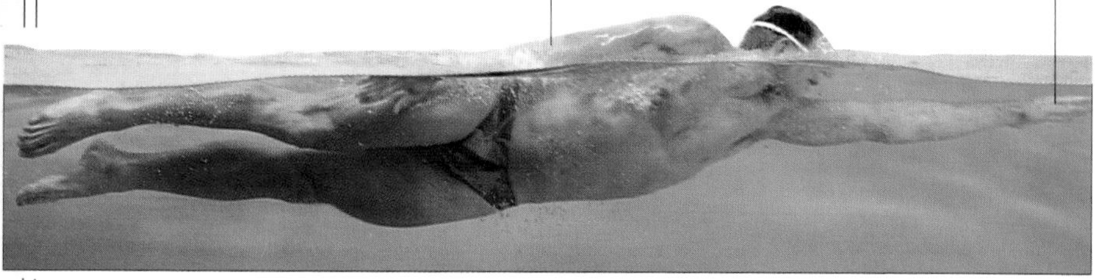

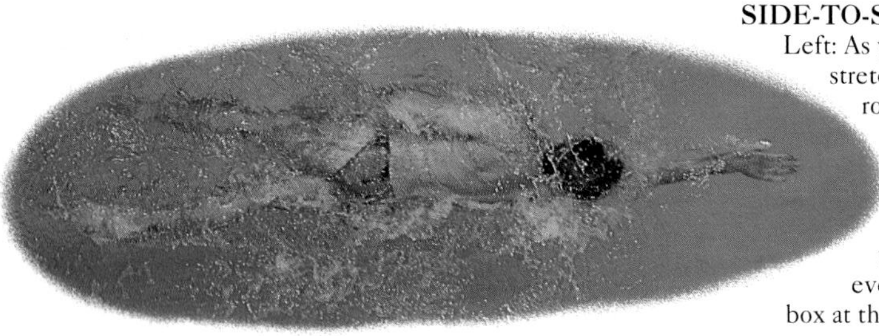

SIDE-TO-SIDE ROLL
Left: As your right arm stretches forwards, roll to the right. You should be inhaling on alternate sides, to keep yourself on an even course (see box at the top of p.55).

MAKE THE MOST OF YOUR STROKE

TOUCH TIP
To ensure that you are doing the full arm stroke, try touching your bottom or the side of your thigh with the hand of your backsweeping arm, before you bring this arm up, out of the water.

GETTING YOUR BREATHING RIGHT

WHEN AND WHERE?
As one arm comes out, the shoulder lifts, and your body rolls to this side (below). Let your head roll to this side, and inhale under your armpit (your face is half out of the water due to a dip in the water caused by a **bow wave** effect from your forward propulsion). This is better than lifting your head up to inhale, which spoils the overall streamlined shape of your body.

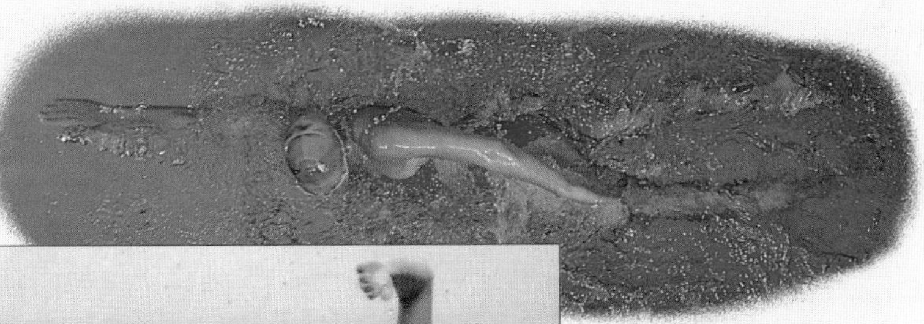

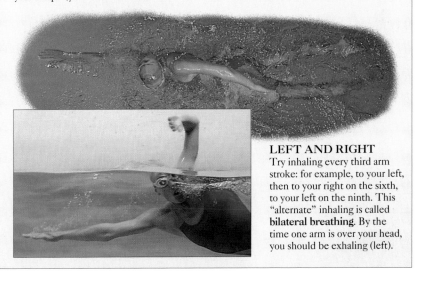

LEFT AND RIGHT
Try inhaling every third arm stroke: for example, to your left, then to your right on the sixth, to your left on the ninth. This "alternate" inhaling is called **bilateral breathing**. By the time one arm is over your head, you should be exhaling (left).

Step 3

INTO THE PULL

As your right arm begins to **recover** above the water, start to **pull** your left arm through the water (with your palm facing backwards), propelling yourself forwards. Lift your right elbow up high. You should be exhaling at this stage.

KEEP YOUR ELBOW HIGH
A high **recovery** elbow at this stage keeps you straight, and stops the arms sweeping round (a waste of energy). To encourage a high elbow, trail recovery fingertips over the surface (as a **drill** only).

HEAD
Look forwards throughout the arm **pull** phase.

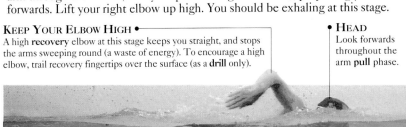

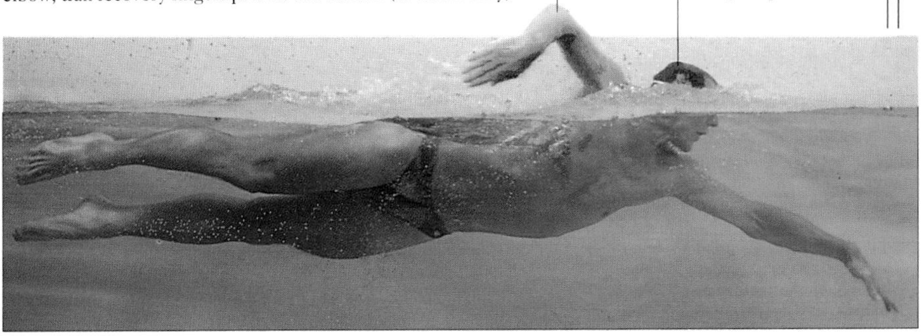

SKILL 6

Step 4

PULLING THROUGH

Pull your working (front) arm back, taking it down deep, as it gets hold of **new water** in order to propel you forwards. Keep this arm **soft**: neither totally straight nor really bent. When it gets to its deepest position, perpendicular to your body, its action should change from a pull to a **push**, as you start to bring it up towards your thigh. Your body should be rolling fully on its axis (see box below). The shoulder of your **recovery** arm should be pulled up fully, and your elbow bent, ready to push your arm forward and down into the water, and so start a completely new arm cycle. Practice watching your recovery hand carefully as it enters the water, so that you can adjust your action, if necessary, on the next stroke.

KEEP KICKING
Keep your legs kicking up and down alternately, with more vigor on the down-kick than on the up-kick.

ARROW-LIKE ENTRY
Your **recovering** hand should enter the water like a streamlined arrow – avoid "slapping" it down.

MAKING AN S-SHAPE WITH YOUR WORKING ARM
This arm makes an S-shape as it **pulls**, then **pushes**, through the water, coming up by your thigh. Viewed from underneath, this is like half the keyhole shape the arms make for the butterfly stroke (half because it's one arm at a time).

FROM SIDE TO SIDE

The body rolls on an axis

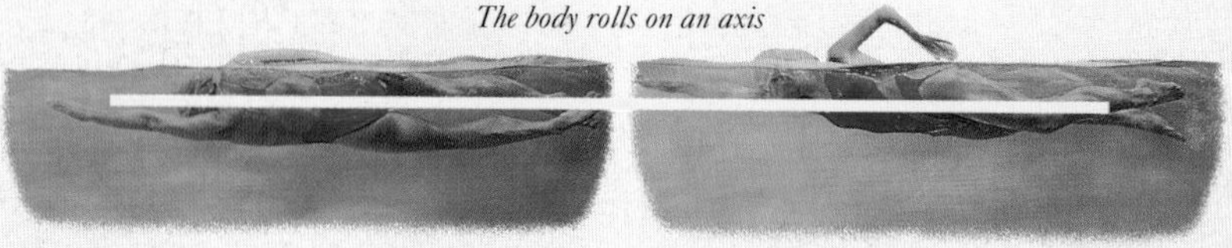

FULL ROLL
You can see above the full extent of the roll – the body is almost on its side. Note how the toes are pointed and how the toes of one foot pass close to those of the other.

RECOVERY AND RE-ENTRY
At this stage, the body is not as tilted. Look forward if possible, as your **recovery** arm re-enters; your other arm is leaving the water, palm up, close to your thigh.

Step 5

STRETCH AND CATCH

Bring your front arm down into the water at full stretch – reach right out in front to find the maximum amount of **new water** to **catch** and **pull**. Start to **recover** the other arm, bringing it out of the water near your thigh, as your shoulder rises with the full body roll. Bring your recovery arm up and over; don't swing it round, over the surface of the water, in too wide an arc.

— *LOOK FORWARDS* —

HEAD ANGLE
Look where you're going, not down at the pool floor, but at a shallower, more horizontal angle, so that you can see your arm enter and **catch** the water.

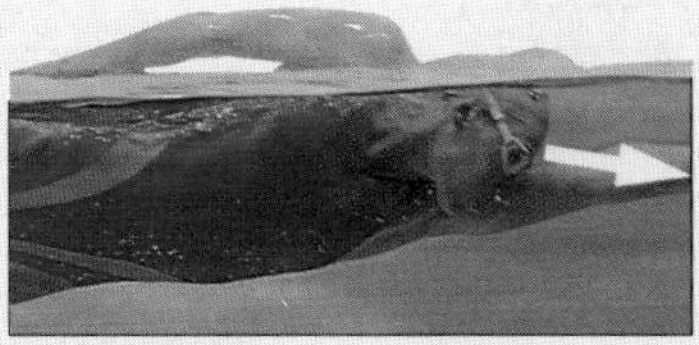

KEEP ROLLING
Notice how the body keeps rolling from side to side on a central axis.

MAXIMUM PADDLE POWER
Remember, your **paddle** is not just your hand, but from your elbow to your fingertips (see p.33).

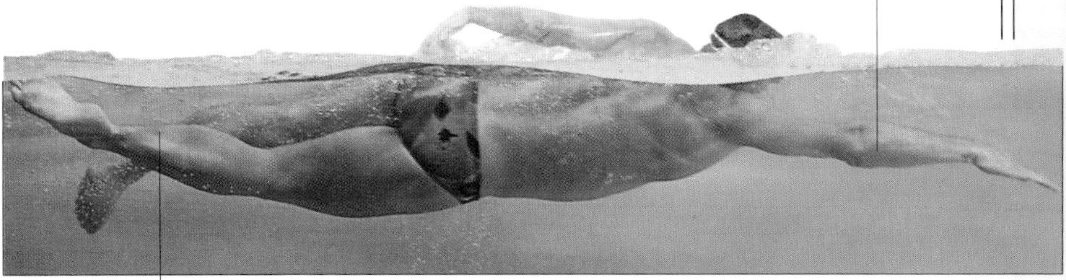

FAST FORWARD WITH YOUR LEGS
Gain speed by increasing the force and frequency of your kick, not just from harder arm **pulls** – keep your arm stroke long and unrushed, if possible.

GO SLOW
This **drill** helps technique by slowing the arm stroke down, and working one arm at a time.

"CATCH-UP" DRILL
Below: As an improvement exercise, try letting one arm catch up with the other.

STAY OUT IN FRONT
Keep this arm outstretched while you bring your **recovery** arm over to join it.

SKILL

6

Legs
Keep your legs going like an engine, with alternate kicks.

Recovering Arm
Your elbow leads your **recovering** arm out of the water, in what should become an automatic action.

ELBOW
Right: Keep your **recovery** elbow high at this stage.

Toes
Keeping your toes pointed creates a larger **paddle**, giving your feet a **flipper**-like action.

In Sequence

For front crawl, your face is in the water, so inhaling at exactly the right moment is vital for timing and rhythm. As you finish one complete arm stroke, you'll have rolled onto one side; your **recovery** shoulder lifts, which turns your face up slightly, ready to inhale, into your armpit. Only half your face needs to be above water for this. Try to bring your mouth, not your whole head, up slightly for the breath and avoid taking in water. As your recovery arm comes further over, get your face back in the water before your recovery hand enters. Once your face is back in, exhale through your nose and mouth.

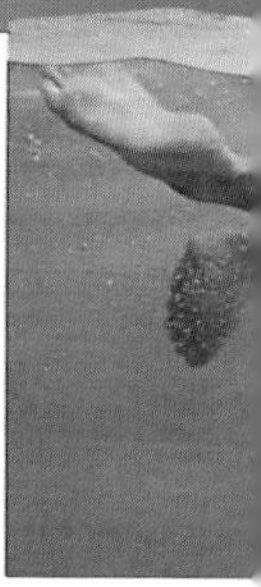

KEEP UP THE PRACTICE
It takes practice to co-ordinate your breathing with your arm and leg strokes, but persevere. Correct breathing also requires practice, and water confidence. Don't rush – an early scare could put you off trying to improve your breathing technique, a technique you must acquire for an efficient stroke.

HEAD POSITION

STAYING ON-COURSE

Your head must be fairly low, with your face in the water, to keep a streamlined shape. Because you must also look where you're going, in order to stay on-course, you may find it more comfortable to wear goggles. The best head position is where the water breaks at mid-forehead (see right) or at your eyebrows. You may like keeping your head even lower, with just the crown above the water. The most important thing is to find a comfortable, streamlined position, where you can see your arm enter and start to **catch** the water.

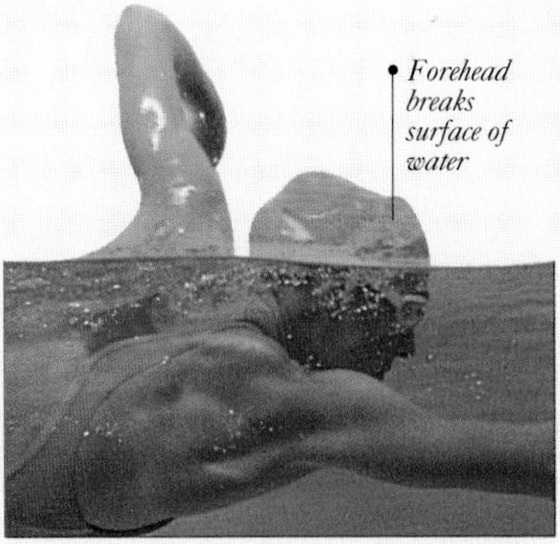
Forehead breaks surface of water

PULLING ARM
Remember, you get greater momentum from your arm **pull** if you use not just your hand, but from your elbow to your fingers, as your **paddle**. Here, the arm is almost half way through its pull action.

POINT OF ENTRY
Watch your hand as it enters the water to check that you have a good action. There should be as little splash as possible when your hand goes in – reserve your energy for stroke-work under the water, for moving the water in the right direction.

HEAD POSITION
Think of your head as a boat's bow: too low and your shoulders rise up and act as brakes; too high, and your body creates drag through the water. Having your head just slightly up makes your body resemble a hydroplaning speedboat thrusting forwards.

SKILL

7 BUTTERFLY

DAY 2

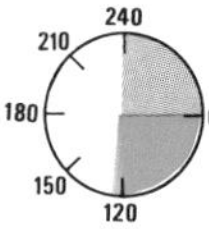

Definition: *An overhead butterfly-like arm action combined with a dolphin-style, synchronized leg kick*

THE BUTTERFLY STROKE resembles the movement of a dolphin through water, characterized as it is by a double-leg, "dolphin" kick. It is the newest stroke, officially recognized only in 1952, and the second fastest stroke after the front crawl. It is also a graceful stroke, but you do need to be strong, and have good timing, as well as the ability to **undulate** through the water.

OBJECTIVE: To **undulate** through the water in a smooth, supple, and controlled fashion. *Rating* •••••

SWIM LIKE A DOLPHIN

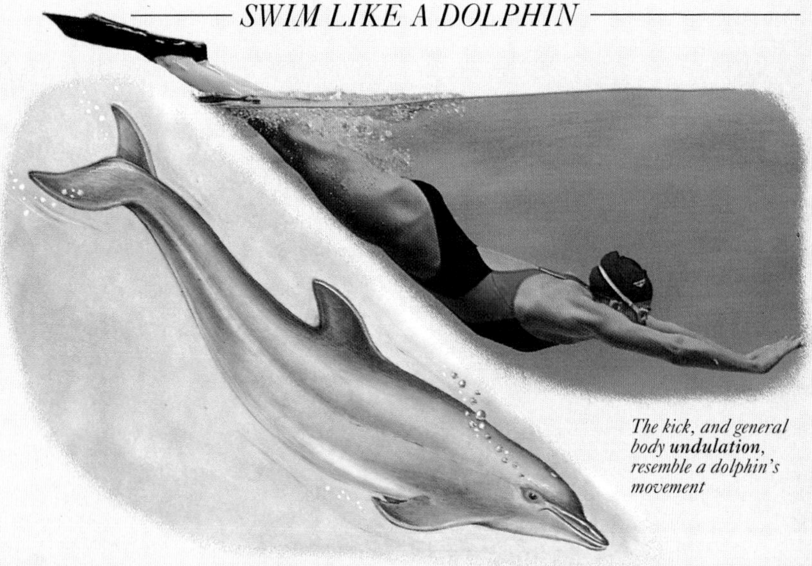

The kick, and general body ***undulation****, resemble a dolphin's movement*

WHIP THROUGH THE WATER

Wearing **flippers** eases you in to butterfly, by enhancing the dolphin-like kick you should aim for. Kick both legs at the same time, working from the hips and bottom, not the knees; press the water with the top of the thighs. The kick is a whip action: the quicker you whip, the faster you move.

BREATHING ON THE 'FLY

It is power in the leg action, rather than in the arm action, that lets you inhale. As flippers enhance your leg-power, they help you to **push** your arms out straight by your thighs and lift yourself out of the water to inhale. The latter is vital: breathing "on the **'fly**" is the stroke's most difficult aspect.

LEG ACTION

WORKING TOGETHER

Your leg action controls your breathing, which in turn controls your stroke's fluency. Work your legs at the same time, not alternately; start your action from the bottom and thighs; and don't over-bend your legs – this pushes water up, not backwards, giving poor thrust. Do two kicks to each arm stroke: a big kick pulls you out of the water to inhale; the second, smaller, kick comes with the arms' **recovery**, and gives balance.

1. Begin to drive your upper legs downwards – this is the start of the first, big, kick. Make sure that both legs are moving together.

2. Don't bend your legs more than this. Now, start to drive your lower legs down; your bottom will rise up.

3. Finish driving your lower legs down, so that you end this powerful first kick with fully extended legs.

4. Start to bring your legs up in preparation for the second kick, which shouldn't be as deep and strong as the first.

5. Lift the legs, ready for the second kick. This kick will *look* bigger than the first, because it's higher, due to the high bottom.

6. Start to drive your upper legs down; your toes emerge from the water as you prepare to kick down with the lower legs.

SKILL 7

ARM ACTION

Step 1

THE ENTRY AND CATCH

Put both arms, shoulder-width apart, into the water in front of your head, ready to start their **pull**. Your head enters the water before your hands. As with all strokes, the best hand position is with fingers relaxed, slightly apart, which creates the widest **paddle**. Slightly parted fingers let the water just slip through; tense fingers, tight together, are too hard to pull through the water easily, and make your paddle too small. Your legs are fairly deep at this stage of the stroke, having just finished the small kick. Remember, the leg action is big kick, little kick, big kick, little kick, and so on.

CHECK YOUR ARM AND HAND POSITION
If possible, keep your elbows above your hands. Angle your hands so that your palms face slightly outwards, ready to start **catching** the water.

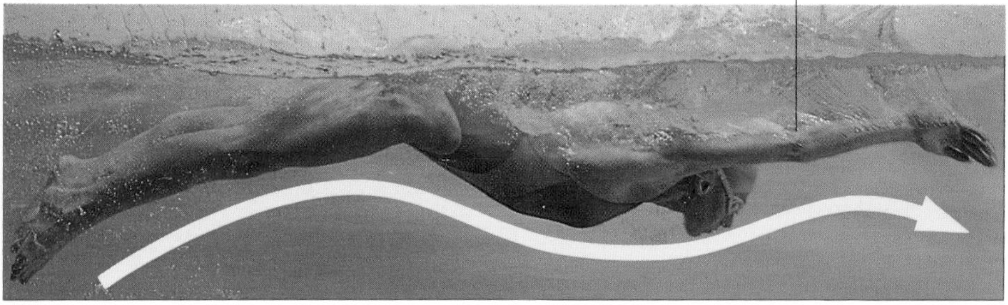

UNDULATION
Swim in a smooth, relatively straight pose, adopting an **undulating**, fish-like movement, similar to a dolphin.

Streamlined, symmetrical body shape

ARMS
Your arms enter together, shoulder-width apart.

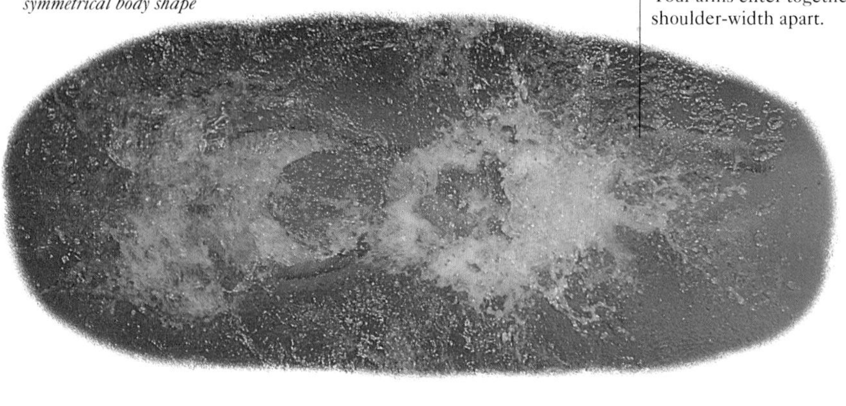

Step 2

PULL AND EXHALE

Pull the arms deep through the water. You are exhaling, through the nose (holding your breath wastes energy). Once past the shoulders, bend the arms slightly to bring them up by your thighs.

Step 3

PUSH AND INHALE

The big kick lifts you up; start inhaling. The arm **pull** becomes a **push**.

ABOVE WATER
Don't raise your head too high to inhale – it will slow you down by spoiling your streamlining. Instead of inhaling on each stroke, you could wait for every second stroke – but you'll need a *lot* of stamina.

• **ARMS**
Pull through strongly. By the end of the pull, you'll be completing the big kick.

BUTTERFLY VARIATIONS

CATCH-UPS
A good way to introduce yourself to the arm action is to move one arm at a time. Put one arm out in front (resting on the surface) and **pull** through with the other, bringing it over to catch up with the front arm. This is easier than the double-arm action, because, instead of pulling yourself up to breathe in, you can breathe to the side, as with the front crawl. Wearing **flippers** will help; you can abandon them as you gain confidence.

LEFT AND RIGHT
Catch-ups are an excellent way to perfect the overall timing of your stroke and they also let you concentrate on your leg kick. However, you can vary this **drill** as you gain in confidence and your technique improves: try doing one catch-up to one side, then one to the other, then the normal stroke with both arms together; or a catch-up on one side, then both arms together, and then a catch-up on the other side.

SKILL 7

Step 4

ARMS OUT

Bring your arms up, out of the water, at the start of their **recovery**. You are still inhaling, and your legs have totally completed the big kick.

Step 5

UP AND OVER

Swing your arms over in an arc, to re-enter the water in front. When your **recovering** arms reach a point roughly level with your head, your head should already be going back down into the water, so that, at the point of entry (see Step 6), your head is in the water.

PLANNING AHEAD • Start to think about putting your head back down in the water.

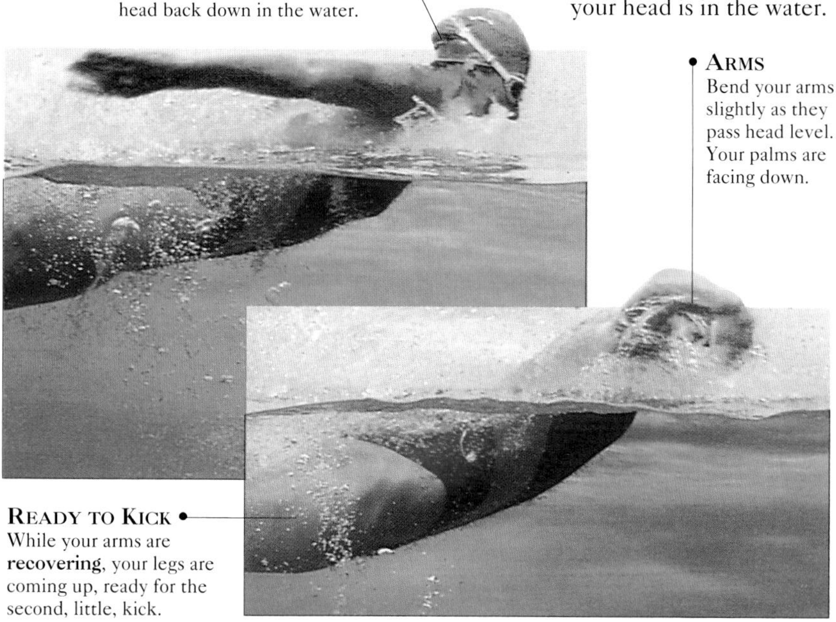

• **ARMS** Bend your arms slightly as they pass head level. Your palms are facing down.

READY TO KICK • While your arms are **recovering**, your legs are coming up, ready for the second, little, kick.

THROUGH THE KEYHOLE

FINDING NEW WATER

To keep finding **new water**, and so maintain momentum, your arms should track this path (right), which forms a keyhole shape when seen from underneath. Enter the arms at shoulder-width; **pull** them down and out; bring them back and in, under your stomach. Your pull changes to a **push** as your hands near your thighs, prior to leaving the water. Your arms arc out and over to their re-entry point in front, ready to start the stroke again.

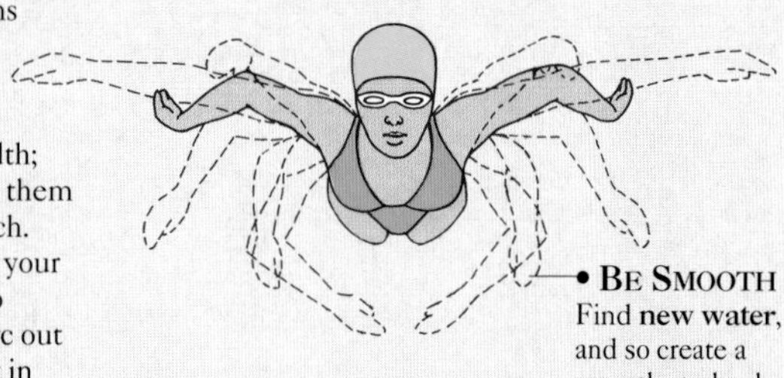

• **BE SMOOTH** Find **new water**, and so create a smooth stroke, by making this track.

Step 6

MAKING A FULL RECOVERY

Recover your arms over the water so that they re-enter, extended, in front of you, ready to start **catching** the water. As the hands approach re-entry, the head should be back down in the water, and you should be beginning to exhale. Move your arms in a fluid shape over the water, neither too bent nor too stiff; bend them gently at the elbow. In mid-recovery, shown overhead below, the elbows should be higher than the hands, and you should be looking at the pool bottom, not forwards.

MAKING TRACKS
This picture shows the path your arms track over the water's surface. They should re-enter in line with your shoulders.

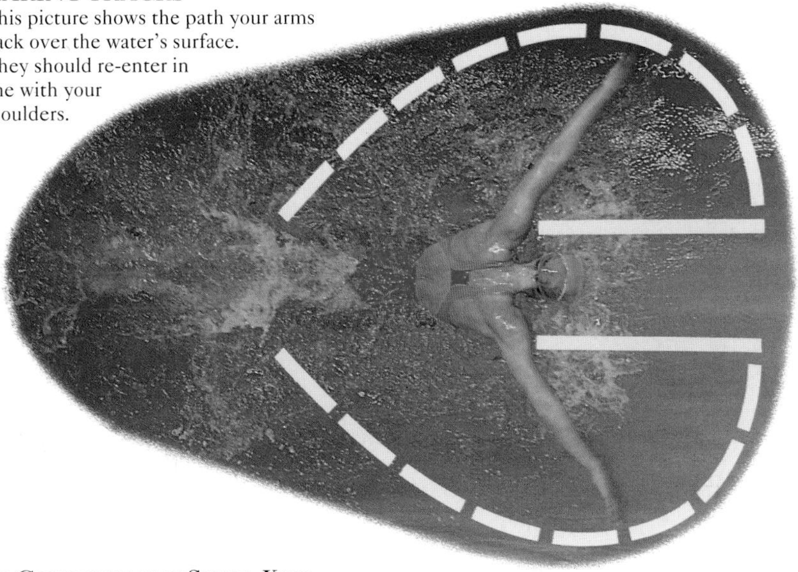

GOING INTO THE SMALL KICK
Every stroke has two stages: a working stage, and a **recovery** stage. Butterfly is no exception – while your arms are recovering over the surface, your legs are kicking to propel you forwards. Here, your bottom is high and your lower legs have just started to drive downwards for the small kick.

SHOULDERS
The power for the arm stroke comes from the shoulder muscles, and the lateral muscles of the back.

The legs stay together as they drive down

SKILL 7

BOTTOM POSITION
In this full-stretch pose, your bottom is high as your legs finish the "small" kick.

READY FOR THE CATCH
Note the out-turned palms, as the hands start to **catch** the water.

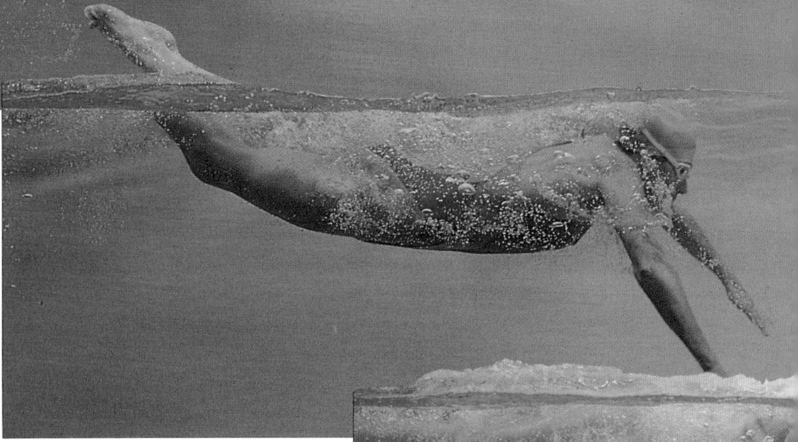

IN SEQUENCE

At first, **'fly** feels clumsy – it takes time to find a fluid, co-ordinated action. Try to **undulate**; jerkiness slows you down, tires you, and looks ugly. A good stroke isn't a matter of brute strength (the water stops you if you rely on that), but of style *combined* with strength. Keep your arms relaxed, not stiff; make them fit in with your legs, not vice versa. Exhale with your face in water; inhale above water. You must be supple for 'fly – try this exercise, at home or by the pool: lie down, on your front, on carpet or a towel. Press down with hands placed under your shoulders, and stretch your back in the kind of arch needed for the butterfly stroke.

KICK
The "big" kick is needed to lift you up, out of the water, to take a breath.

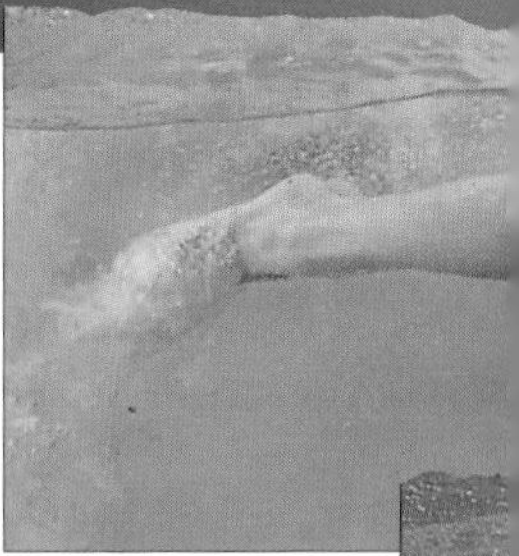

LEG POSITION
Don't worry whether or not your legs are close together at any point of the stroke (if they do become close together, it will probably be at the end of the stroke).

STARTING TO FINISH

LOOKING FROM ABOVE

This overhead view – at the end of the big kick, with arms about to **recover**, and head up to inhale – shows the symmetry you need. If you imagine a line down the center of the body, one side should mirror the other.

SHOULDER FLEXIBILITY

The shoulders may feel tense at the stage shown below – it's an awkward pose. As soon as you've inhaled, and started to lower your head, the tension should stop. You need flexible shoulders for **'fly**, especially for arm recovery.

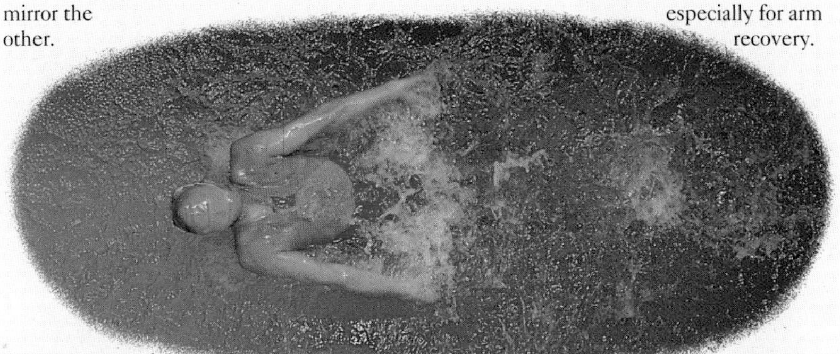

THE SEQUENCE

The small kick ends as the hands start to catch. The arms pull, as you finish exhaling. This pull becomes a push as the big kick lifts you up to inhale. Your arms recover as you start the small kick. Full recovery is a resting pose, with the small kick still pushing you forwards.

• **HEAD**
The head is clear, ready to take a breath. Look forwards, not at the pool bottom.

• **STOMACH**
It helps to have quite strong stomach muscles. Feel them work as you whip up and down.

• **RECOVERING ARMS**
On **recovery**, the arms are just slightly bent. Bring them round in a fairly wide arc (not too wide). Keep the hands **soft**.

• **FACE AND HEAD**
Your head is back in the water (it enters before your hands), ready to start the **stroke cycle** all over again.

SKILL

DAY 2

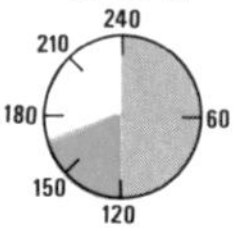

8 Taking Turns

Definition: *Techniques, used in competitive* ***backstroke*** *and front crawl, for turning around at the pool wall*

In competition, you need to change direction at the pool wall quickly and efficiently. There are special turns for all the strokes, governed by specific rules – Skill 8 covers the simple **flip turns** used for the front crawl and **backstroke**; other racing turns are shown on pages 84-85. When racing, don't slow up as you approach the wall. Think of a tennis ball: if you hit it slowly against a wall, it comes back slowly; hit it hard and it returns with full speed.

OBJECTIVE: Changing direction correctly and effectively. *Rating* •••••

Front Crawl Flip Turn

1. Getting Used to Flipping

Develop your front crawl turn one stage at a time. Begin by simply practicing turning front somersaults in shallow water, away from the wall, starting from a standing position. Don't worry too much about your finishing position. Now repeat, but concentrate on ending up on your back, legs fully extended.

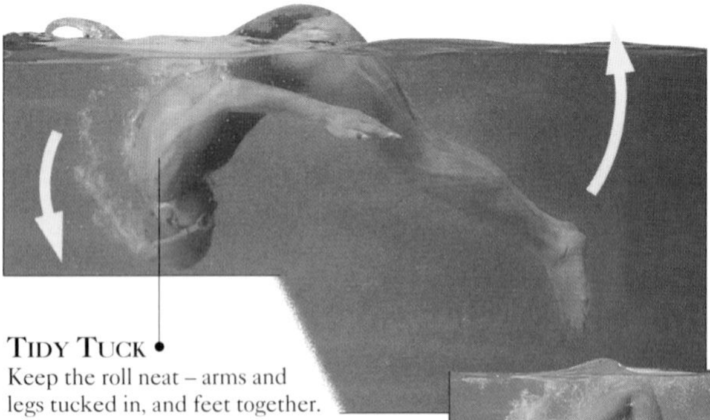

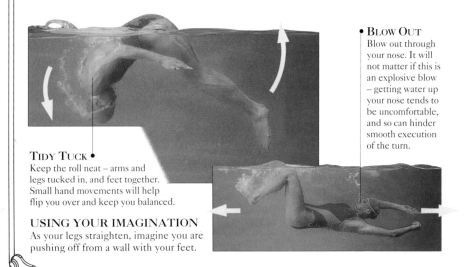

Blow Out
Blow out through your nose. It will not matter if this is an explosive blow – getting water up your nose tends to be uncomfortable, and so can hinder smooth execution of the turn.

Tidy Tuck
Keep the roll neat – arms and legs tucked in, and feet together. Small hand movements will help flip you over and keep you balanced.

USING YOUR IMAGINATION
As your legs straighten, imagine you are pushing off from a wall with your feet.

2. ROLL AND PUSH

Repeat the roll, but closer to the pool wall, so that your feet are planted on the wall, and push you off into the outstretched position on your back. Aim to be about half-an-arm's length away from the wall as you plant your feet. Don't rush – you'll need plenty of practice to judge the distance you must be from the wall as you roll forwards, and to place your feet correctly.

ARMS
Stay streamlined, ready to **glide** on your back, with arms outstretched above your head. Don't **pull** with your arms.

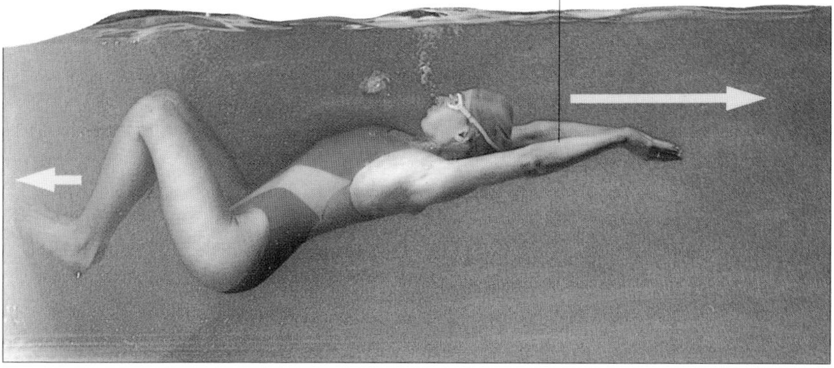

3. ONTO YOUR FRONT

Try the roll again, but this time, as you push away from the wall on your back, twist round 180°, ready to swim away on your front. Keep your arms in front, as streamlined as possible. When you feel your **glide** fade, start the front crawl kick. Don't begin the arm **pull** yet; that would raise your shoulders, "burying" the front of your body, and so bringing you to a halt.

INTO THE FINAL STRETCH
As your feet push you off forcefully from the wall, your legs should straighten right out, before starting the front crawl leg action.

ALL IN ONE
Push off and roll onto your front in one fluid, continuous movement; don't push off on your back and then roll round onto your front.

SKILL 8

LEGS
As you approach the wall, and drive your head down, keep your legs together, just under the surface of the water, and as parallel to the surface as possible. Try not to let your legs drop down.

HEAD
Don't drive your head down too deep. Keep it tucked in: you should look towards your feet.

FLIP
As your feet and legs emerge from the water, flip them over quickly, ready to plant your feet on the wall.

TWISTING
Once you are well-practiced, aim to start twisting slightly as soon as you begin to flip your feet over, so that you aren't totally on your back when you push off from the pool wall.

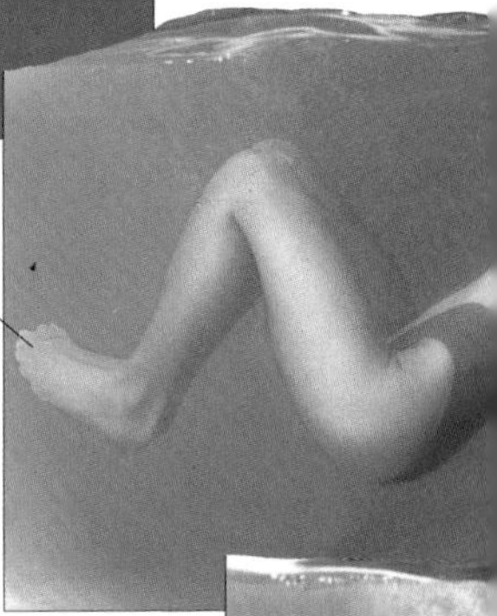

PLANT AND PUSH OFF
If you plant your feet too low on the wall, you'll push off diagonally, up towards the surface. Too high, and you'll head for the bottom. Push off a little way under the surface.

IN SEQUENCE

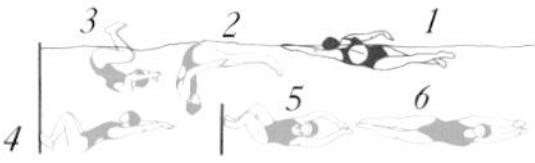

This full sequence shows how smooth the front crawl **flip turn** should be. As you near the wall, doing the front crawl, drive your head down strongly, and flip your legs over. Don't slow down, or you won't have enough speed to bounce back off the wall, and don't stick your head up just before you flip over – this makes you lose your streamlining and so puts the brakes on. Instead, look through the water to see how far you are from the wall. Coming up for breath immediately after the turn also slows you down, so wait until your second or third front crawl stroke.

NO HANDS
While your feet must touch the wall for the front crawl **flip turn**, your hands needn't touch it at any stage.

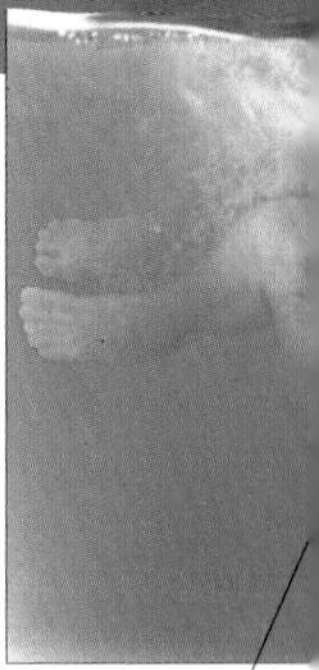

TWISTING
You are starting to twist round, ready to swim off on your front. As you improve, try going straight from Step 3 to Step 5 – so, as you begin to flip over, you are also starting to turn onto your side. This means that, by the time you push off from the wall, you are on your side, ready to turn onto your front.

ARRIVALS AND DEPARTURES

1. INTO THE TURN
Start the turn when the front hand is about half-an-arm's length (half a full arm stroke) from the wall (below). Look at the point where you'll plant your feet. Take a good breath as the other arm goes up and over, and follow it down. As you enter the **flip**, exhale through the nose.

2. AFTER THE TURN
Make the most of the **glide** from the push-off. Learn to judge when the glide is slowing down, then start kicking hard, and then **pulling** with your arms. Hold your breath for the first couple of front crawl strokes, then come up to the surface to breathe.

GET IT STRAIGHT
Left: This photograph shows clearly how planting your feet on the wall at the correct height positions you so that you push off in a fairly straight line. At first, you will find it easier to come off the wall on your back, as shown. But this can slow you down, which is why top competitors will already have turned 90° by the time their feet hit the wall.

• HANDS
Keep your hands **soft** throughout the turn, particularly as you twist from your back to your side.

• STREAMLINED ARMS
If you can feel your ears against your shoulders, you know that your arms are in the correct streamlined position for a good **glide**.

SKILL 8

BACKSTROKE FLIP TURN

Step 1

GET READY

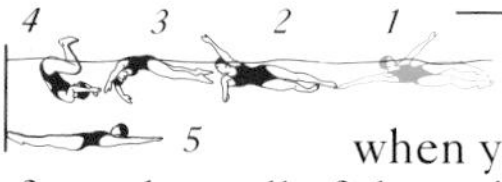

Start thinking about the turn when you are three to four arm strokes from the wall of the swimming pool. In competitions, there are usually flags at this distance. In the absence of flags, you could pick a specific point on the ceiling, or count how many arm strokes you do in one length of the pool – it is your last arm stroke that will take you into the turn.

• UP AND OVER
Having left the water, this arm will come up, across your body, and lead you into the turn.

Steps 2 and 3

INTO THE ROLL

Continue to bring up whichever arm started rising out of the water in Step 1 (on your last arm stroke before the wall). However, instead of bringing this arm back down into the water in line with your shoulder, as with normal **backstroke**, bring it across your body as you roll onto your front, ready to go into a forward **flip** (see Step 4). Take a deep breath as the roll momentarily exposes your face.

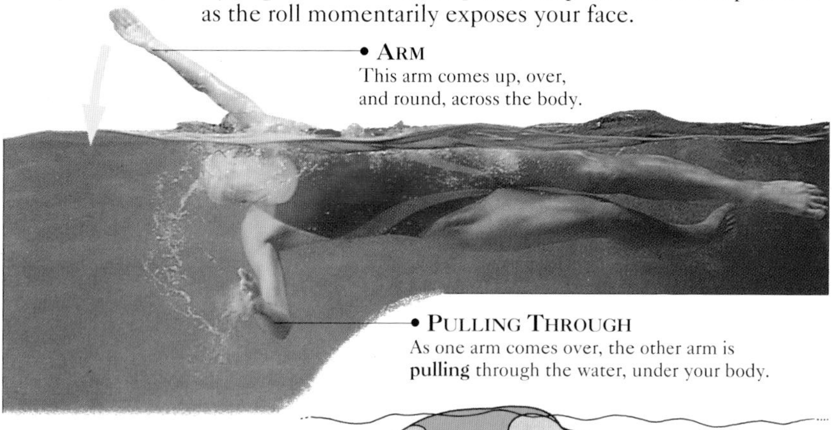

• ARM
This arm comes up, over, and round, across the body.

• PULLING THROUGH
As one arm comes over, the other arm is **pulling** through the water, under your body.

READY TO FLIP
Once on your front, you are ready for a forwards **flip**. Aim to bring the arm over, roll, and flip in one continuous, fluid movement. Keep your head tucked in as you roll.

Step 4

FORWARDS FLIP

As you roll onto your front, go into a neat forwards **flip**, as you did for the front crawl turn. Hold your breath as you flip. Position yourself in such a way that, as you emerge from the flip, your feet are brought down and planted on the wall, ready to push you off, on your back.

THE RULES

CHANGING TIMES

The style and rules for the **backstroke** turn have changed drastically over recent years. The old turn was very different because you had to touch the wall with your hands on every turn. Now, you touch with your feet only. You must also roll onto your front when you are one stroke away from the wall, in a continuous movement – if you roll onto your front, then put an arm stroke in, and then **flip** forwards, you will be disqualified.

KEEP LEGS TOGETHER Make sure that both legs move together, neatly, as you **flip**.

Step 5

PUSHING OFF

Let your legs take the strain as your feet push you off from the wall. You should be exhaling by the time you push off. The force of the push-off gives you the momentum to **glide**, fully stretched, on your back for a few moments. As soon as you begin to feel your glide slow down, start the **backstroke** leg kick. This kick brings you to the surface, ready to start the arm action and inhale again. There isn't an "In Sequence" feature for this turn, as it is all shown on these two pages.

Arrow-like arms help make the most of the ***glide***

SKILL 9

DIVING IN

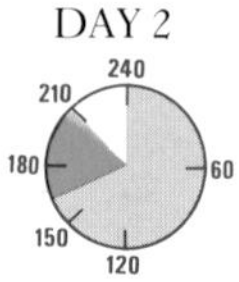

Definition: *Entering the water head-first, from the poolside*

DIVING CAN SEEM a daunting skill to tackle from scratch, so build it up in stages. Pages 74-75 show a basic "plunge dive" (or "standing dive"). The "In Sequence" feature on pp.76-77 builds on this, adding extra steps to create a simple dive that provides perfect groundwork for those who want to go on to master a full racing dive (see pp.78-81). Before diving, you *must* check that the water is deep enough – at least 1.5m (5ft); depths should be marked on the poolside. Only dive in pools: it is difficult to judge the depth of rivers or the ocean. Don't attempt dives other than those shown in Skills 9 and 10 without an instructor's help.

OBJECTIVE: A neat entry, with a minimum of splash. *Rating* ••••

"PLUNGE" DIVE

Step 1

INTO POSITION

Stand at the pool edge, and extend your arms forwards, as shown. Make sure that you are relaxed – you mustn't tense up before you dive. Try to imagine a "hole" in the water ahead, and aim to put yourself through this hole when you dive in.

The arms have been omitted so that the feet can be seen

OVERVIEW
Standing at the poolside, keep your feet about hip-width apart, with your toes curled over the edge. This gives you a stable "platform" from which to dive.

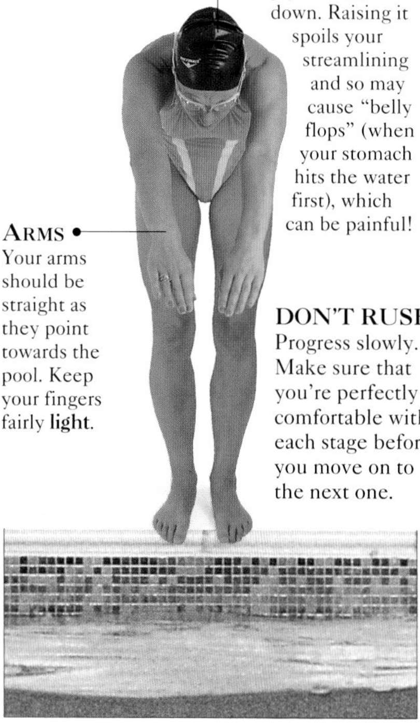

HEAD
Keep your head down. Raising it spoils your streamlining and so may cause "belly flops" (when your stomach hits the water first), which can be painful!

ARMS
Your arms should be straight as they point towards the pool. Keep your fingers fairly **light**.

DON'T RUSH
Progress slowly. Make sure that you're perfectly comfortable with each stage before you move on to the next one.

BASIC DIVES

HEAD
Keep your head tucked in. Aim to feel your ears against your arms.

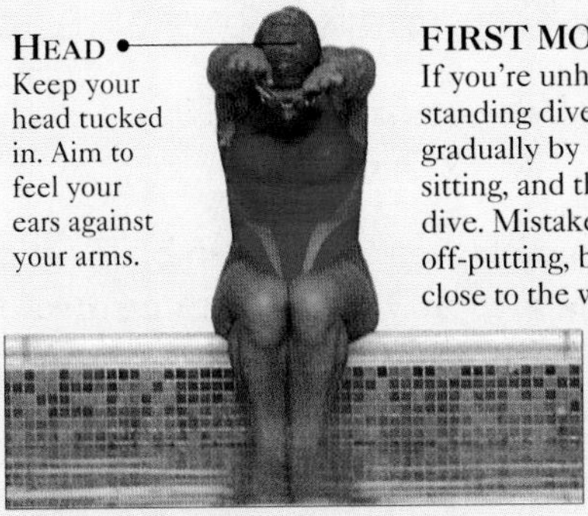

FIRST MOVES
If you're unhappy doing a standing dive, lead into it gradually by first trying a sitting, and then a crouching, dive. Mistakes won't be so off-putting, because you are close to the water.

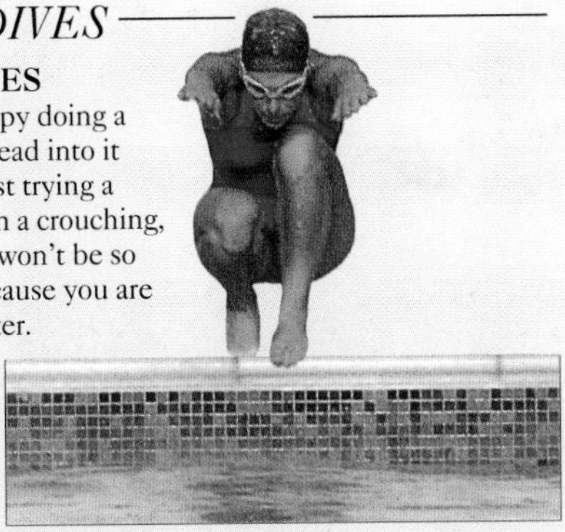

SITTING DIVE
Sit on the side of the swimming pool, with your knees together, and your feet over the edge. Point your arms forwards, as shown, and tip your body into the water, aiming to put all of it through a specific "hole" that you have picked out.

CROUCHING DIVE
Squat down (or kneel with one knee), point your arms, and tip forwards, into the water. Thrust powerfully with your legs to improve your streamlining. This helps to make up for the poor entry angle caused by having bent legs.

Step 2

INTO THE WATER

With your head between your arms, "fall" gracefully into the hole that you picked out in Step 1, fingers first, then wrists, elbows, head, shoulders, and then the rest of your body. At first, pick a hole close to the poolside; as you improve, aim for a spot further out, pushing harder with your feet to get there. Keep your hands firm (not rigid). To help you resurface after the dive, point the fingers upwards.

ARROW
From fingertips down to toes, feel your body as streamlined as an arrow as you dive. Tuck your head in so that you feel your ears touching your arms.

SPLASH
Aim to minimize the water splash on entry. You should try to dive through the water, rather than "hit" it.

SKILL
9

FULL DIVE

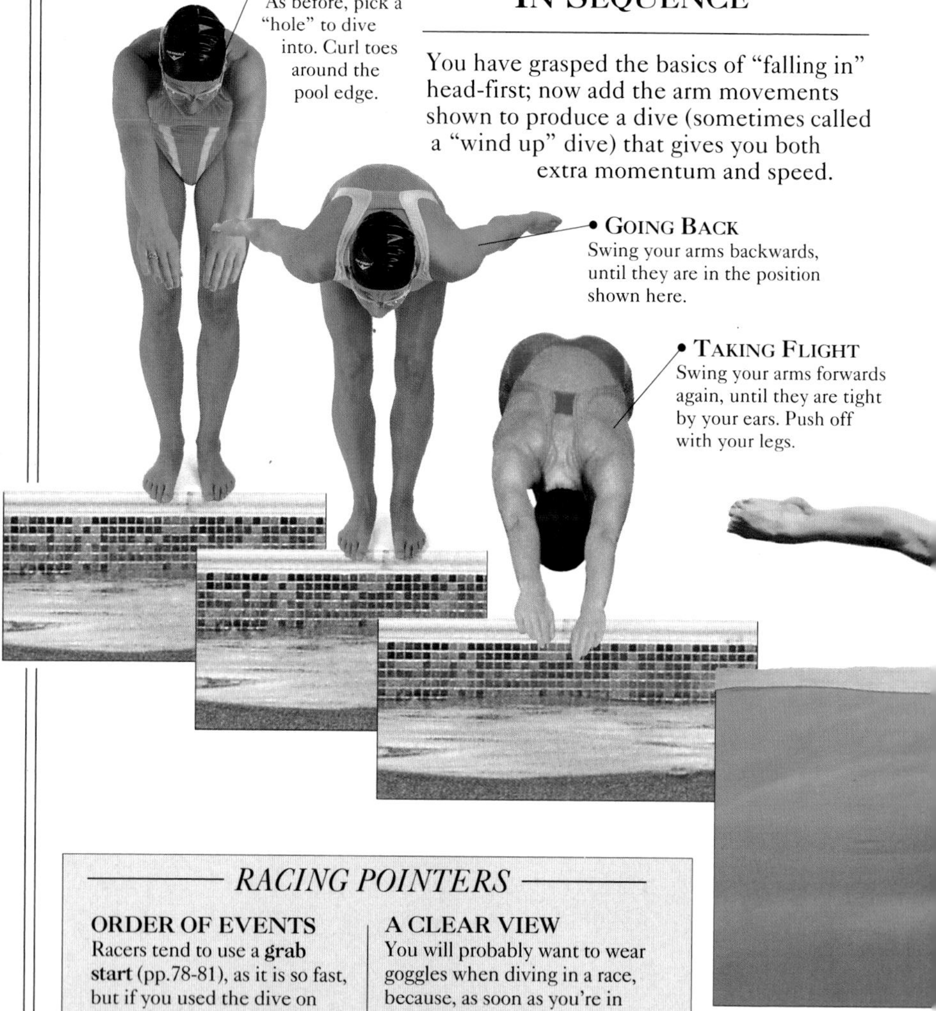

LOOK OUT
As before, pick a "hole" to dive into. Curl toes around the pool edge.

IN SEQUENCE

You have grasped the basics of "falling in" head-first; now add the arm movements shown to produce a dive (sometimes called a "wind up" dive) that gives you both extra momentum and speed.

GOING BACK
Swing your arms backwards, until they are in the position shown here.

TAKING FLIGHT
Swing your arms forwards again, until they are tight by your ears. Push off with your legs.

RACING POINTERS

ORDER OF EVENTS
Racers tend to use a **grab start** (pp.78-81), as it is so fast, but if you used the dive on these pages in a race, the sequence would work as follows:
• On the "Take Your Marks" signal, swing your arms back.
• On the "Go" command, sweep your arms forwards. When they are tight by your ears, push off. The body and head have lowered, but don't lose sight of the "hole".

A CLEAR VIEW
You will probably want to wear goggles when diving in a race, because, as soon as you're in the water, you must be able to see exactly where you are. Diving in goggles takes practice: they can come off quite easily. Adjust the strap until they are secure, but comfortable. Keep your head down: lifting it can dislodge goggles. Wear a cap to keep your hair out of your face.

SMALL STEPS
You should make sure that you feel absolutely happy with this dive before you progress to the racing start shown on pages 78-81.

INTO THE HOLE

HIT THE WATER CORRECTLY

If your body enters the water in a totally straight position, the back part of it will be outside the hole that you should be trying to dive through (shown clearly below). To counteract this, lift your bottom a little, angling your body slightly.

... BY INCREASING THE ANGLE

As increasing your angle of entry ensures that your whole body dives through the hole, it reduces water splash. Minimal splash shows that you are also cutting down water **resistance**. A slightly angled entry also makes the dive deeper and faster.

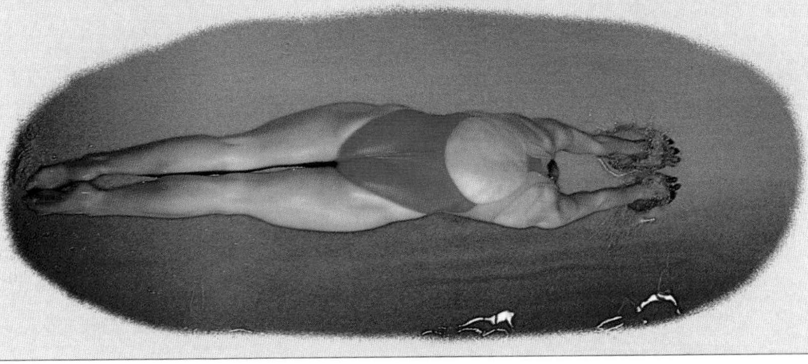

THROUGH THE HOLE
During your **flight**, you should have angled your body slightly so that, as you enter the water, you put your whole body – from fingertips to toes – through the hole you have been fixing your sights on.

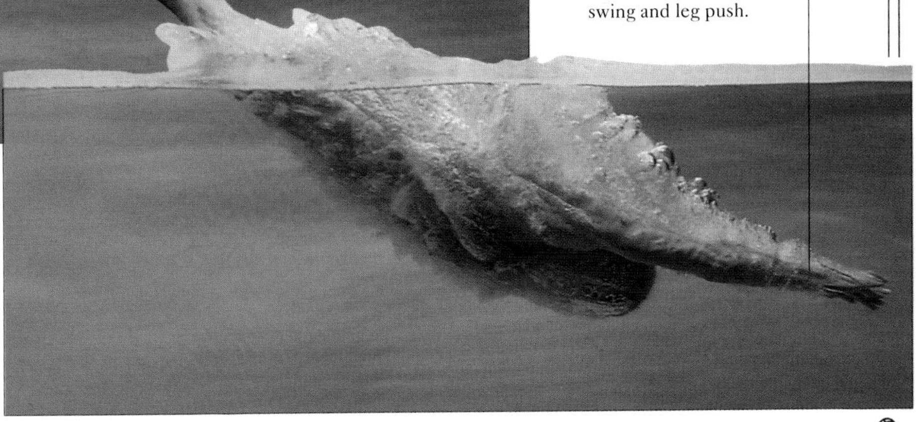

USING YOUR GLIDE
As you straighten right out in the water, make the most of your **glide**. The glide is given more momentum by the arm swing and leg push.

SKILL

10 RACING START

DAY 2

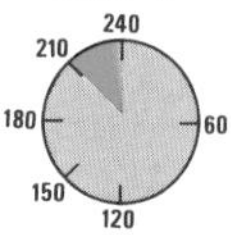

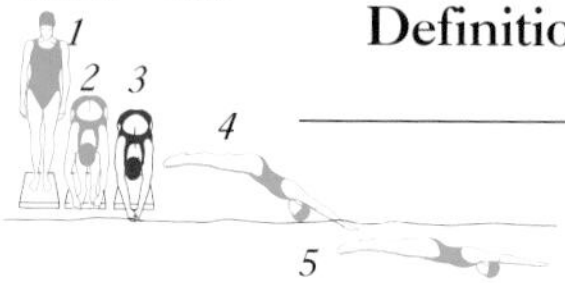

Definition: *A* ***grab-start*** *dive, used in races*

DIVING FOR A RACE is all about getting off to a rapid start that takes you as far down the pool as possible. A **grab start** is a highly effective way of achieving this when diving forwards, as you use your arm muscles for extra power.

OBJECTIVE: To gain speed in the air, and **gliding** momentum in the water. *Rating* ••••

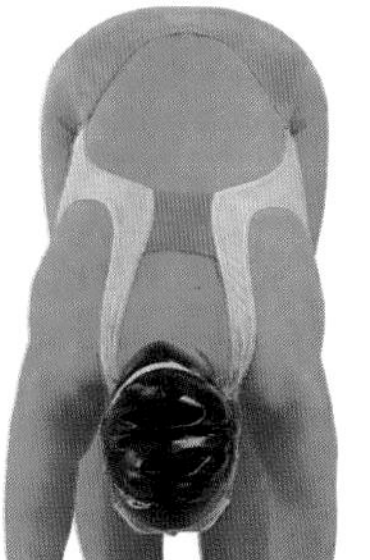

Step 2

READY TO SPRING

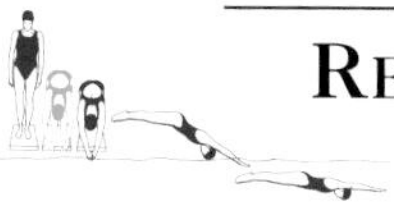

Having started off standing behind the **block**, you will – on a signal from the referee – have mounted the back of the block. At the "Take Your Marks" signal, take up the position shown here, at the front of the block, with your hands holding the edge, and your knees bent. Curl your toes over the edge of the block, so that you gain enough grip to work your leg muscles strongly when you spring off into full **flight**.

• **HANDS**
Your hands can be either over the front of your feet, or on either side of your feet – choose whichever feels most comfortable.

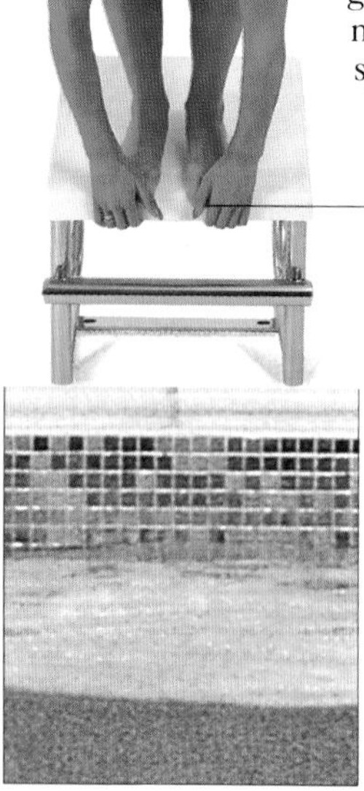

RELAX
Keep practicing until you feel relaxed and comfortable in this position.

• **LIKE A SPRING**
You should feel coiled up, like a spring ready to be released.

STARTING BLOCKS
Above: This side-on view shows how standing on the kind of **block** used in races gives you extra height and a deeper angle – adding speed and distance to your dive.

Step 4

DIVING IN

On hearing the official "Go" signal, you have left the **starting block** as follows: pull up with your arms as your body overbalances forwards. As your knees bend further, your arms swing forwards (at which point your head comes up and you can see the "hole" that you're aiming to dive into). Push off with your legs and feet. Bend your body as you leave the block. This ensures that your whole body dives through the chosen hole, giving you greater speed on entry, and good momentum to your **glide** once you're under the water.

SECRET OF SUCCESS
The key to a good dive is to keep your limbs together and your head tucked in snugly between your arms, forming a completely streamlined shape.

HIPS AND BOTTOM
Lifting your hips and bottom brings your feet up, so that all of your body goes through the hole you've picked, encountering the minimum water **resistance**.

BACKSTROKE START

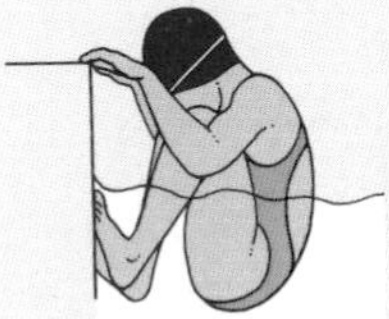

1. IN A COIL
At the "Take Your Marks" signal, pull yourself up into a tightly sprung, coiled position, ready to spring back into the dive.

2. "GO"
On hearing the "Go" signal, pull your weight up with your arms. Push hard with your feet and legs.

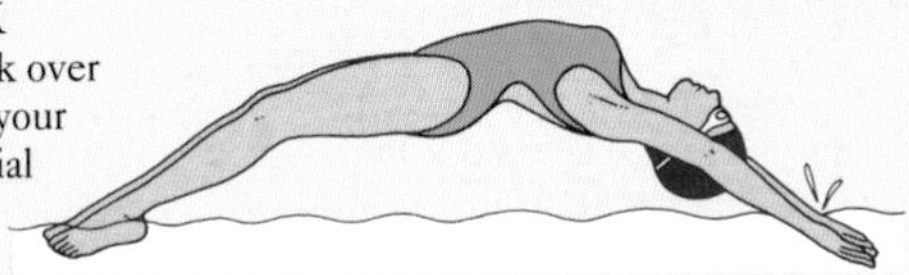

3. GOING BACK
Fling your arms back over your head. Arching your body gives your initial **glide** depth and speed.

CLOSE TO THE SURFACE
The technique shown here provides a speedy, "sprung" start for **backstroke** races, using arm-power in the same kind of way as for the **grab start**. Place your feet as high as possible, to give a strong push-out. However, in competitive events, although your toes can be right up to the surface, they must be seen to be under it. Once in the water, when the **glide** fades, you can do two or three butterfly kicks before starting the backstroke kick – this gives you a powerful start.

SKILL
10

IN SEQUENCE

For competitive racing starts, you need to be aware of the rules and procedures, as well as the skills themselves – there is a fine line between gaining maximum advantage in the **grab start**, and being disqualified for a false start. Listen for the starting signal – you don't have to look – but don't try to anticipate it. The rules state that only one false start is allowed – by any of the competitors in a specific event; after that, any infringement of the rules means being disqualified.

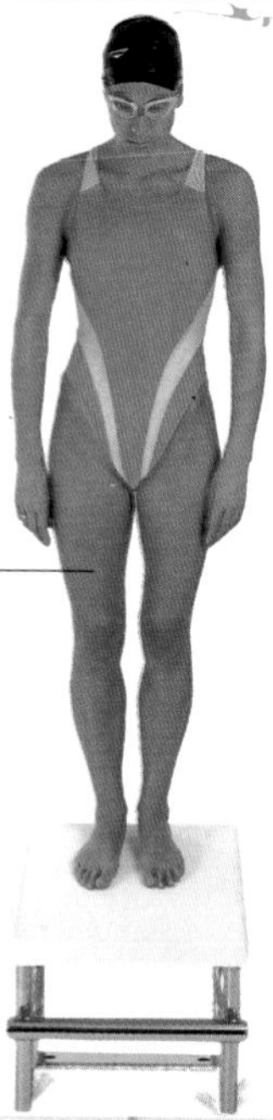

START • You start off standing behind the **block**. When you hear a signal, get up onto the back of the block.

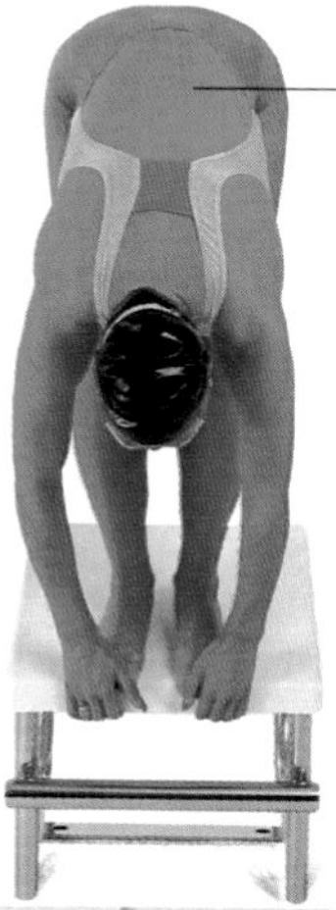

GRAB POSITION On hearing "Take Your Marks", move to the front of the **block**, and go into the **grab start** position. You must keep absolutely still at this stage – the slightest twitch could disqualify you.

Arched body shape

BREATHING

GOING WITH THE GLIDE

Avoid coming up to the surface to inhale on the first stroke that you take after coming out of the dive. This is because lifting your head to take a breath tends to put the brakes on, so try to stay down for the first stroke. In breaststroke, you're allowed one kick and one arm **pull** under the water before surfacing; you must surface by the time you're on your second stroke.

HEAD LIKE A RUDDER

Notice how your head acts like a boat's rudder: keeping it low as you dive in sends you deep into the water. Once underwater, bringing your head up to see where you're going also brings your body up; continue to raise it to bring yourself up to the surface.

MAINTAINING POWER

AFTER THE DIVE

You will need to keep your momentum going powerfully as you come out of your dive. This is so that you don't grind to a halt before you begin whichever stroke it is that you are doing.

GLIDE, LOOK AHEAD, KICK

Once you are in the water, you should always try to make the most of the speed and force of your **glide** – don't start kicking with your legs immediately, as this tends to create drag and so slows you down. Only start to kick when you feel your glide begin to slow down. In fact, the first thing that you should do when you feel your glide start to fade is to lift your head up far enough to see where you are going, and *then* start a powerful kicking motion, working your legs hard like a little "engine" (see the photograph on the left).

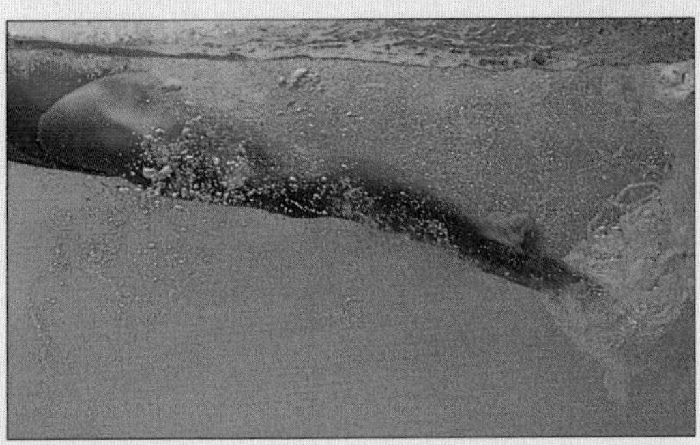

"GO" – INTO FULL FLIGHT

On hearing the electronic "Go" signal, pull hard on the front of the **block** with your hands and overbalance forwards, into the dive. Raise your hips to arch your body so that all of it enters with minimum splash. The **grab start** is so efficient because all the movement is forwards, whereas there is a slight backwards momentum half way through the "wind-up" dive (see pp.76-77).

THE GLIDE

Once you've dived in, make the most of your **glide** through the water. Keep your arms together, and your fingers pointed – but not stiff.

AFTER THE WEEKEND

From water skills to water sports

BEING ABLE TO SWIM opens up so many enjoyable activities – sailing, windsurfing, jet skiing ... (see p.15, *Learn to Sail in a Weekend* and *Learn Windsurfing in a Weekend*). Once you have mastered the essentials of this course, you can try these out for yourself, even taking them to competition level if you wish.

But swimming is also an excellent all-round activity in itself – it's especially good for promoting general fitness, flexibility, and strength. Develop a good technique, and go swimming regularly, and you will soon feel your health benefit (see p.14).

Think about joining a club – your local pool probably has one that is open to all ages. If you have a swimming skill that you want to try out competitively, ask about Masters Swimming. Anyone over 25 can enter Masters events – you don't need a qualifying time, you just need to belong to a club. Enquire at your local pool, or contact U.S. Masters Swimming (see p.96).

To maintain your fitness and technique, try to do at least two, half-hour sessions each week. Early morning or lunch-time are generally quieter times, and a swim at these times tones you up for the rest of the day. "Early-starter" clubs are a great way to begin the day, meet people, and, if you're aiming to enter long-distance events, tot up a weekly distance. Check at your local pool for details. Many pools also run classes in water **aerobics** – a great way to keep both fit and trim (see pp.88-89).

Whether you swim for gentle recreation, competition, or to learn another water activity, set yourself realistic targets – and do your best to stick to them (see pp.20-21, 90-91).

MEDLEY SWIMMING

Putting all your skills together

MEDLEY SWIMMING, the "pentathlon" of water events, is swimming's toughest challenge. It incorporates everything you have learned – all four strokes, plus turns, starts, and finishes, and more. Even if you don't want to swim it competitively, it is an excellent way to practice all your skills.

Grab-start *racing dive* *(see pp.78-81)*

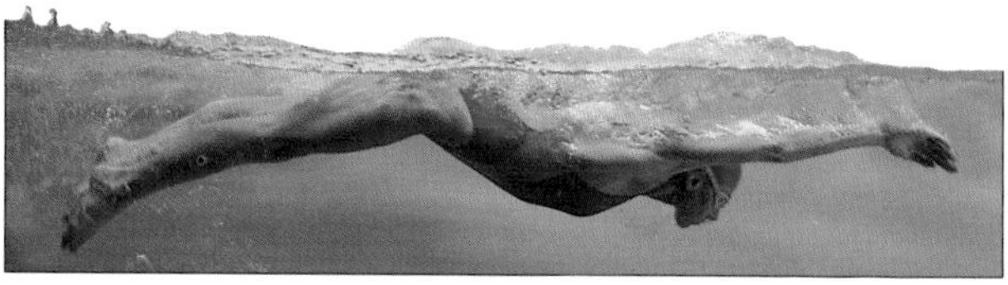

FIRST STROKE: BUTTERFLY

Twist round full circle (use your touching hand as a lever)

THIRD STROKE: BREASTSTROKE

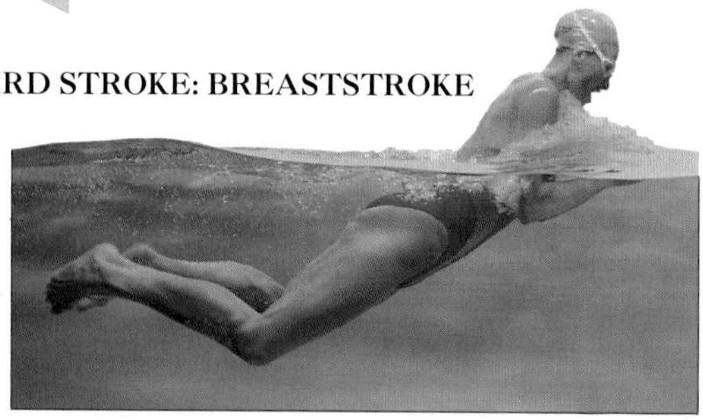

BACKSTROKE TO BREASTSTROKE TURN

Coming in on your back, reach behind and touch the wall with one hand. You are allowed one underwater arm **pull** and one kick as you touch. Twist your body round so that your feet push you off from the wall, on your front.

Pool wall

CHANGEOVERS

Medley swimming is particularly demanding because you have to switch from swimming on your front to your back, and from fast to slower strokes. To change from one stroke to another smoothly, you need to use the special turns that are shown on these two pages. In competition, these turns are subject to strict rules, some of which are outlined in the text.

RULES AND REGULATIONS

ORDER OF EVENTS

In "individual medley" events, a competitor swims equal distances of four strokes, in the following order:

- butterfly
- **backstroke**
- breaststroke
- front crawl.

Swimmers must follow all the competition rules for each of the strokes.

INDIVIDUAL AND RELAY

- There are two individual medley events: 200m and 400m – 50m or 100m of each stroke (in a 25-m pool, use normal stroke turns part-way through a stretch).
- There is also a 4x100m relay medley, for which the stroke order is: **backstroke**, breaststroke, butterfly, front crawl. Your feet mustn't leave the **starting block** until your relay partner has touched the wall.

BUTTERFLY TO BACKSTROKE TURN

Touch with both hands (they must touch horizontally level), bring your knees up towards your stomach, and throw your upper body back. Push off from the wall with your feet, ready to swim away on your back.

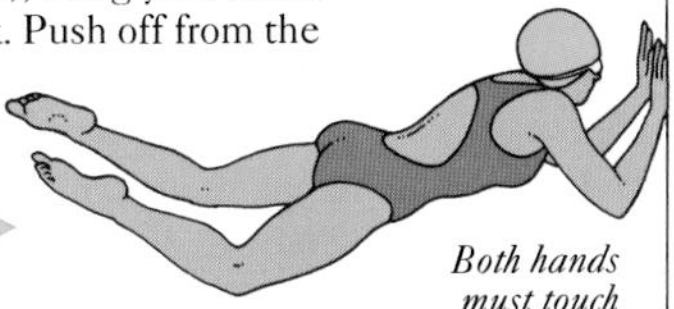

Both hands must touch simultaneously

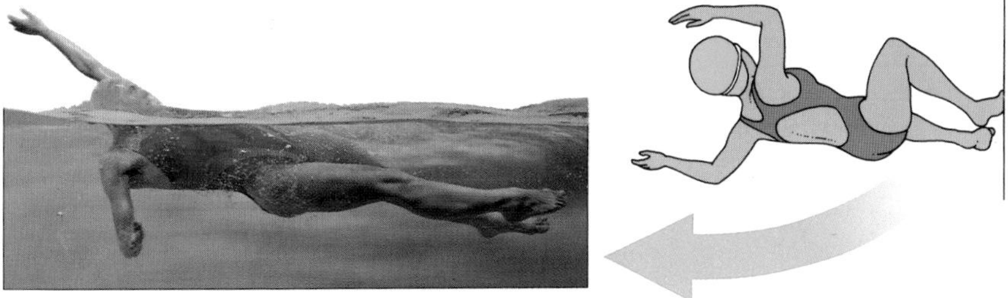

SECOND STROKE: BACKSTROKE

Basically, this is also the way you would turn for breaststroke and 'fly races

BREASTSTROKE TO FRONT CRAWL TURN

Both hands touch simultaneously, hands and shoulders horizontally level. Bending your knees, bring one hand towards your ribs, and the other over the surface, and down into the water, followed by your head.

Twist so that your feet push you off from the wall as you move onto your front

FINISHING STROKE: FRONT CRAWL

BASIC WATER SAFETY

Some simple procedures for dealing with difficulties

SWIMMING IS NOT JUST a sport – it is a fundamental life-saving skill. If you see someone in difficulty in water, your first thought might well be to try to save them by jumping in. This is actually the last option you should choose. Someone panicking in water has a tremendous strength, and is likely to pull you down as he or she struggles. The best thing to do, whether you are the rescuer or the rescued, is to stay as calm as possible, and try the procedures shown here. You don't need to be strong; a small child can rescue an adult using these methods.

TOWING IN

This is the first option that you should try if someone struggling in water is fairly close to the poolside, or water's edge. Coil up a rope – or a towel or pair of trousers; it's unlikely that a rope will be to hand – and throw it to the swimmer. Do it calmly, so that you get it right first time – a soaked object is much more awkward to drag back in and throw out again accurately.

BALANCED POSITION Lie by the side. Make sure that you are in a well-balanced and secure position, so that you can't be pulled into the water.
GRIP Always use something that you can both grip well.

KEEP TALKING

If a swimmer is further out, throw them a **float**. Tell them to kick their legs, and keep their head above water. You will reassure them if you stay calm, and talk to them all the time. Use beckoning gestures and encouraging words such as: "I'm here, swim to me, I'm waiting for you."

WHAT TO USE •
If a buoyancy **aid** isn't handy, use a ball, or a plastic drinks bottle.

IN THE WATER

THE LAST RESCUE RESORT

Rescuing a swimmer by getting into the water yourself should be a last resort. Using a vertical version of breaststroke kick to stay afloat, get the swimmer onto their back, in a floating position. Hold their face above water by putting your hand over the center of their chin (keep it clear of the throat), and try to get them to kick. Offer the swimmer constant verbal reassurance.

GAINING CONFIDENCE

WATER GAMES

Anything that makes you more relaxed in and around water is helpful – playing underwater games is an excellent way of doing this. Games can help to:

• make you safer and less likely to panic if anything goes wrong. Games can also:

• break up the monotony of simply swimming lengths;

• give enjoyable exercise to those with special needs that make other forms of exercise difficult, such as asthmatics and those with physical handicaps or sports injuries;

• introduce beginners to moving in water (provided they are happy being immersed), and help those needing a way to get used to underwater swimming.

GAMES IDEAS

Try making up your own games, based on popular ones such as:

• picking up hoops from the pool floor and throwing hoops over sticks (see below);
• swimming through pool hula hoops;
• doing handstands on the pool bottom;
• swimming through a friend's legs;
• diving and retrieving objects from the bottom of the pool.

WATER AEROBICS

Aerobic exercise** in the water, working against water's natural **resistance

WATER **AEROBICS** TONES THE BODY and exercises a wide range of muscles by working the body against the **resistance** of the water. The natural support of the water keeps any stresses or strains to a minimum. Try these routines as a pre-swim warm-up, or to add variety to your training program; water aerobics is also valuable for those recovering from injury, older people who want to keep supple, and pre- and post-natal women. Take it as gently as you like; the routines shown here are basic, introductory ones.

Ideally, the pool should be warm. Stand where the water comes up roughly to shoulder height, and preferably close to the side of the pool, in case you need support. Many swimming pools run water aerobics classes, usually accompanied by music, making them shared, fun-with-fitness sessions.

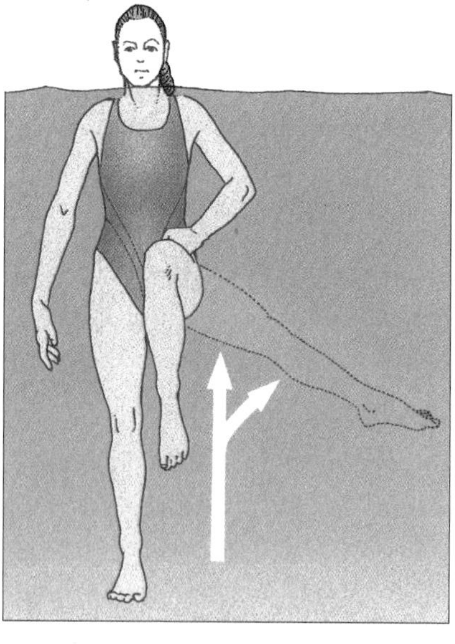

1. THIGHS

This tones the front and inside of the thighs. Lift one knee towards your chest, then lower the leg, and swing it out sideways. Do this ten times, then repeat with the other leg. Do the exercise holding onto the poolside rail if you don't feel confident about your balance.

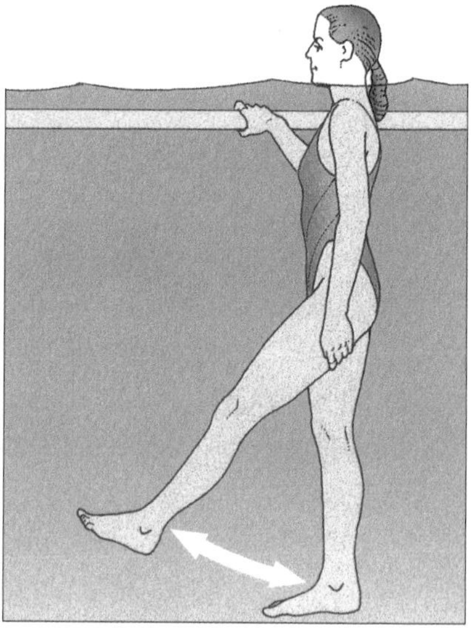

2. THIGHS AND BACK

Good for the buttocks, upper thighs, and lower back. Swing one leg back and forth ten times, shallowly and slowly; keep your back straight and your standing leg slightly bent at the knee. Switch to the other leg. Now repeat, but hold the rail and swing higher and more vigorously.

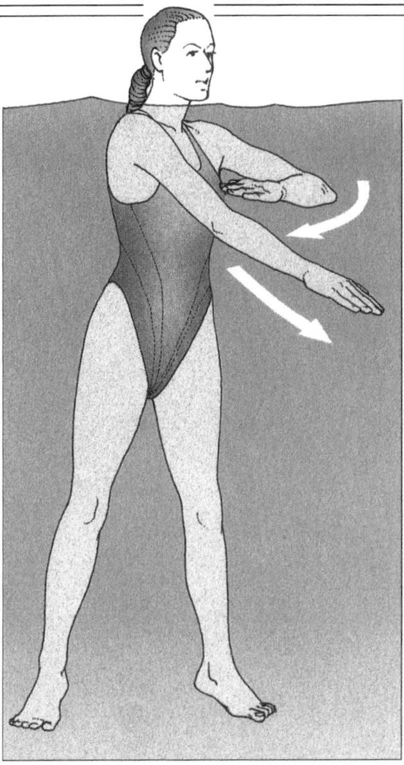

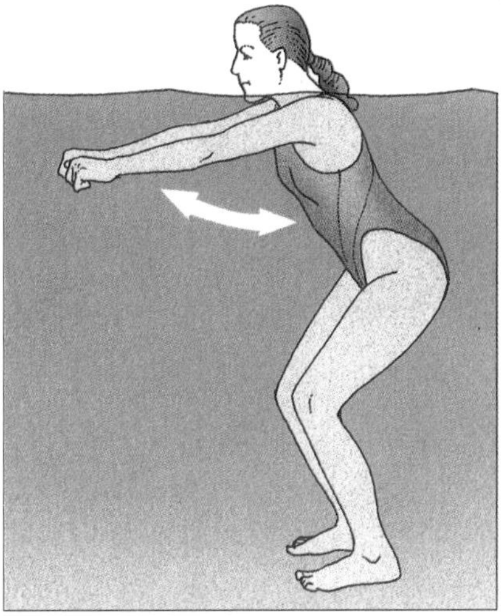

3. ARMS AND SHOULDERS (above)
Bend the knees. With extended arms, and clenched fists, pull 15 times, in a rowing action.

4. ARMS AND WAIST (left)
Raise your arms to just below shoulder height, bent at the elbow. Swinging your body from one side to the other, punch down with alternate arms as you turn (ten punches each arm).

"HYDRO-FIT"

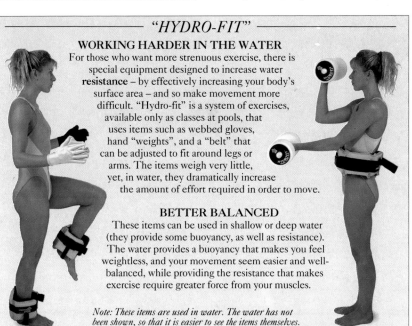

WORKING HARDER IN THE WATER

For those who want more strenuous exercise, there is special equipment designed to increase water **resistance** – by effectively increasing your body's surface area – and so make movement more difficult. "Hydro-fit" is a system of exercises, available only as classes at pools, that uses items such as webbed gloves, hand "weights", and a "belt" that can be adjusted to fit around legs or arms. The items weigh very little, yet, in water, they dramatically increase the amount of effort required in order to move.

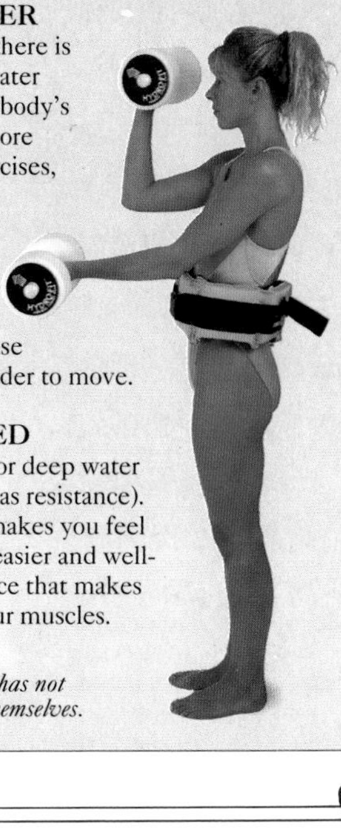

BETTER BALANCED

These items can be used in shallow or deep water (they provide some buoyancy, as well as resistance). The water provides a buoyancy that makes you feel weightless, and your movement seem easier and well-balanced, while providing the resistance that makes exercise require greater force from your muscles.

Note: These items are used in water. The water has not been shown, so that it is easier to see the items themselves.

TAKING IT FURTHER

Getting serious about your swimming

YOU MAY FIND THAT you want to build up your fitness by taking your recreational swimming relatively seriously. You might decide to progress to local club events, or go even further and aim for the highest competitive levels. At any of these levels, you will need to devise a suitable training schedule (see opposite page), and choose the right kind of pool. Fortunately, most pools rope off lanes for swimmers who want to swim lengths in order to improve their stamina, endurance, or speed. Follow any signs telling you which direction to swim in – clockwise or counter-clockwise – so that you don't bump into other swimmers, and stick to the lane put aside for your ability: slow, medium, or fast.

COMPETITION SWIMMING
An Olympic standard swimming pool, such as the one shown above, has eight lanes. The ropes used to separate pools into lanes help to prevent wave turbulence from one lane disturbing swimmers in the next.

IN TRAINING
"Circle" swimming – several swimmers going up and down a lane in a clockwise or counter-clockwise direction – is what competitive swimmers do when training together. Tailor training to your personal needs (see opposite).

HOW FIT ARE YOU ?

Monitor your fitness by checking how quickly your heart rate returns to normal after exertion (the fitter you are, the quicker it returns). For example, do a rapid 100m of a stroke. Press two or three fingers lightly over the wrist pulse point (right) and count the beats for 15 seconds. Multiply this by four, to give a rate per minute. Repeat 30 seconds later, and 30 seconds after that, to assess how fast you return to a "resting" rate – around 80 beats per minute.

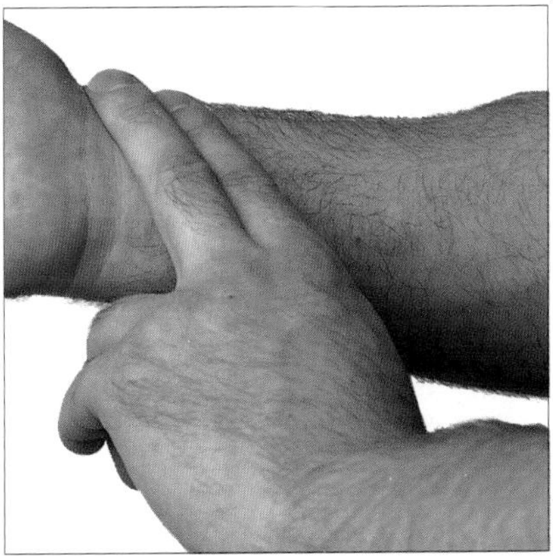

YOUR PERSONAL PROGRAM

GOOD PLANNING

If you are aiming for any competitive level, you must plan a sensible training schedule that includes a "warm-up", a "main set", and a "cool-down".

FROM FIT TO SUPER-FIT

Use the three sample programs below to devise one that suits you. Take your pulse regularly to monitor your fitness, and watch the poolside clock to check your speed.

	Distance	Type/pace of stroke	Total distance
		EASY SESSION	
Warm-up	200m	any stroke, steady pace	200m
Main set	16x25m	front crawl; 15 seconds rest every 25m	400m
	200m	leg action best stroke (arms use **floats**)	200m
	200m	arm action best stroke (legs use floats)	200m
Cool-down	200m	any stroke	200m
			TOTAL 1200m
		MEDIUM SESSION	
Warm-up	3x200m	front crawl, steady pace; 60 secs rest every 200m	600m
Main set	8x50m	leg action best stroke (arms use floats); 15-30 secs rest every 50m	400m
	8x50m	arm action best stroke (legs use floats); 15-30 secs rest every 50m	400m
	8x50m	any leg or arm **drill**, complete stroke, or combination; 15-30 secs rest/50m	400m
Cool-down	200m	any stroke	200m
			TOTAL 2000m
		HARD SESSION	
Warm-up	2x400m	any stroke, steady pace; 30 secs rest every 400m	800m
	3x200m	individual medley (see pp.84-85): 200m leg action, 200m arm action, 200m complete strokes; 15 secs rest every 200m; steady pace	600m
Main set	6x100m	50m best stroke arm drill + 50m complete best stroke; 30 secs rest every 100m	600m
	8x50m	front crawl leg action (arms extended), hard pace; 20 secs rest every 50m	400m
	6x50m	front crawl arm action (legs extended), hard pace; 15 secs rest every 50m	300m
	4x50m	front crawl, complete stroke, hard pace; 10 secs rest every 50m	200m
		now take a reasonable rest (at least 2 mins) to prepare for the timed 100m	
	100m	front crawl, complete stroke, very hard pace; timed for speed	100m
Cool-down	200m	any stroke, easy pace	200m
			TOTAL 3200m

Note: Most reasonably sized pools are 25m (80ft) long

GLOSSARY

Words in *italic* are glossary entries.

A

• **Aerobic exercise** Long-duration exercise that requires a continuous supply of oxygen; for example, water aerobics (see pp.88-89). ("Anaerobic exercise" refers to any form of exercise that requires less oxygen – for example, short swim sprints.)
• **Aids** Any object, usually buoyant, that helps swimmers to get used to moving around in the water, or to isolate and so practice either an arm or a leg movement.

B

• **Backstroke** An alternating stroke that is performed on your back. It may also be referred to as the back crawl, due to its similarities to the front crawl.
• **Bilateral breathing** Breathing first to one side, and then to the other, on every third arm stroke.
• **Block** See *Starting block.*
• **Bow wave** A wall of water in front of the head created when moving at speed. It also creates a "trough" (which follows the wave), where fast front crawl swimmers can take a breath.

C

• **Catch** The moment when the hand starts to exert pressure on the water during an arm stroke.

D

• **Density** A swimmer's (or an object's) weight in relationship to his or her size.
• **Drill** Practice exercises to improve specific aspects of technique.

F

• **Flex** Another term for "bend".
• **Flight** The part of a dive that takes place in the air.
• **Flip turn** A fast way of turning at the pool wall, during *backstroke* and front crawl races, which involves a forward roll or somersault.
• **Flippers** Rubber or other synthetic "extension" for the feet, particularly useful for providing a power boost when doing swimming *drills*. Flippers are often called "fins".
• **Float** A buoyancy and *drill aid*, made of polystyrene or a similar synthetic material.
• **'Fly** Increasingly accepted shorthand for the butterfly stroke.
• **Freestyle** A freestyle event is one where a competitor can choose any stroke. Front crawl is usually chosen, as it is the fastest stroke, and so the two terms are often used synonymously.

G

• **Glide** Streamlined, arrow-like position as the body moves through the water, with no leg or arm action. Gliding is critical after *flip turns*, dives, and in the breaststroke *recovery* phase.
• **Grab start** A fast racing start where a diver pushes off from the *starting block* with the hands as well as the feet.

K

• **Kickboard** (also called "kick *float*") A rectangular shaped float; useful for holding onto with your arms in order to isolate your legs for swimming *drills*.

L

• **Light** See *Soft*.

N

• **New water** The fresh areas of water that your arms and your legs must keep finding and moving in order to keep your momentum going.

O

• **Oxygen deficit** A temporary shortage of oxygen in the body, created by exertion. With practice, your body will learn to cope with less oxygen when you are swimming.

P

• **Paddle** Your arm, from your hand to your elbow. *Sculling* teaches you to make the most of your paddle.
• **Pull** The part of an arm action, starting with the *catch*, and ending at shoulder level, that pulls you through the water.
• **Pull-buoy** A *float* held between the legs in order to isolate and practice any arm action. It gets its name from the fact that the part of the arm stroke that most effectively propels you through the water is the arm *pull*.
• **Push** The part of the arm action after the *pull* and before *recovery*.

R

• **Recovery** The part of either an arm action or a leg action that provides no propulsion, and returns the arms or legs to their starting position.
• **Resistance** How water acts against the solid mass of a swimmer's body and slows down their progress.

S

• **Screw kick** Unsymmetrical and ineffective breaststroke leg action.
• **Sculling** Small inwards and outwards movements with the hands and arms (and/or the legs). Sculling is often used in synchronized swimming.
• **Soft** Relaxed, as opposed to tense and rigid.
• **Starting block** A raised pedestal at the pool edge, off which competitors dive at the start of a race.
• **Stroke cycle** One complete arm and leg action in any stroke.

U

• **Undulation** A rhythmic and co-ordinated movement of the whole body, rather like that of a fish.

W

• **Wedge kick** An optional breaststroke leg action; wider than a *whip kick*.
• **Whip kick** Whip-like breaststroke kick action that creates low *resistance* and high propulsion.

TOP TEN

Ten Key Rules of Competitive Swimming

1. Only one false start is allowed across all the pool lanes (that is, one false start by any of the competitors in a specific event). Any subsequent infringements, by any competitor, will automatically disqualify that competitor.
2. When turning and finishing during breaststroke and butterfly events, both hands must touch the wall, and be horizontally level as they touch.
3. Competitive breaststroke has to be symmetrical. A *screw kick* will automatically disqualify you.
4. You cannot turn off your back when you are swimming *backstroke*, except as part of turning at the pool wall.
5. At no time in any race can you actually walk on the bottom of the pool.
6. In *freestyle* races, you must stick to your chosen stroke throughout.
7. Your feet must be under the water's surface for the *backstroke* start.
8. For the breaststroke start and turn you are allowed one underwater stroke.
9. In relay races, the previous swimmer must touch the wall before the next swimmer can dive in.
10. Medley racing has to consist of the four recognized strokes. Competitors must do an equal distance of each stroke, and swim the strokes in the correct sequence (see pp.84-85).

INDEX

GETTING IN TOUCH

U.S. Swimming
1750 East Boulder
Colorado Springs, CO
80909
Tel. 719-578-4578

U.S. Masters Swimming
2 Peter Avenue
Rutland, MA
01543
Tel. 508-886-6631

ACKNOWLEDGMENTS

James Harrison is a writer and editor with many years' experience of working on a wide range of information books and magazines, and a particular interest in sport. **Rosa Gallop**, The British Swimming Coaches Association Omega Female Coach of the Year, 1990, has extensive experience of teaching all ages and abilities.

Sharron Davies and Dorling Kindersley would like to thank the following for their help in the production of this book:

Robin Brew and Lissa Davies for modelling. Chris Stevens, for his excellent split-level photography, and the photo-shoot support team: Tony and Tim Tarleton (photography assistants), John Griffin (set builder and engineer), Andrew Schofield (diver). Dave Robinson for helping to set up photography. Mr and Mrs Moore at York House School, Rickmansworth, for the use of their pool for the main photographic sessions. Mrs Offer, for the use of her swimming pool for test photography. Archway Pool, London, for providing us with the location for photos on pp.12 & 14. The Finals (a division of Andmore Sportswear Corporation, Matlock, Derbyshire), Lillywhites (Piccadilly Circus, London), Hydro-fit Incorporated (Oregon, USA), and Racco Products Ltd (Sheffield), for loaning swimwear and equipment.

Linda Dadd, for her advice on water aerobics; Heather Dewhurst for proof-reading; Lol Henderson for editorial assistance and Hilary Bird for the index. Arthur Brown, Janos Marffy, Coral Mula, Sandra Pond, Jim Robins, and John Woodcock, for illustrations.

All photography by Chris Stevens, except for: pp. 74, 76 (first two images), 78, 80, 84 (first image), 89: photography by Jo Foord. Also: All-Sport (UK) Ltd: Beverly Williams 15bl, Tony Duffy 90b; J.Allan Cash Ltd: 13b; Lupe Cunha: 12c, 12br, 14t, 14bl; Philip Gatward, DK: 15tr; Malvin van Gelderen: 13t; Susan Griggs Agency Ltd: Julian Nieman 14br; The Image Bank: Chuck Fishman 15tl, Larry J.Pierce 15cl, Paul Slaughter 15cr, Co Rentmeister 15br; Spectrum Colour Library: 33t; John Walmsley Photo Library: 13c. (t=top, b=bottom, r=right, l=left, c=center)